Royal Doulton Series Ware

Volume 2

In a Man's World
Feminine Society
Travel through the Ages
Life on the Ocean Wave
Rural England
Sport & Leisure

LOUISE IRVINE

RICHARD DENNIS
London 1984

ROYAL DOULTON SERIES WARE

Design and Phototypesetting by Flaydemouse
Photography by Colin Jeffrey Associates and
Prudence Cumming Associates
Printed in Great Britain by Edwin Snell printers
Babylon Hill Yeovil Somerset BA21 5BT
Published and distributed by Richard Dennis
144 Kensington Church Street, London W8

ISBN 0 903685 14 0

Acknowledgements

I am deeply indebted to Royal Doulton Tableware
Limited for permission to reproduce material from
their archives, and for their generous cooperation
in the preparation of this book.

I should like to thank the author, Louise Irvine,
for her particular dedication and expertise, and
Jill Rumsey for writing the section introductions.

Additional thanks are due to Desmond Eyles,
John Jenkins, Jocelyn Lukins, Stephen Nunn,
Caroline Wilkinson and Marguerita Trevelyan-Clark.

RD
January 1984

Contents

Introduction to Volume 2

This book is the second on the subject of Series ware, the name applied to an assortment of decorative and practical items, such as plates, vases or jugs, which are printed with popular imagery. Volume One was concerned with series inspired by literature, historical events and popular illustrators. This volume continues the study of a now flourishing collecting field by recording all the series depicting Olde Worlde Imagery.

There are a great many series which fall into this category because Charles Noke, the Art Director who introduced Series wares in 1900, had an astute awareness of his public's taste and appreciated their strong nostalgic tendencies. It seems that even the Victorians and Edwardians, who are often viewed romantically today, wore rose coloured spectacles to help them escape from their grimy industrial surroundings.

Members of the Arts and Crafts movement found solace in the Medieval period and helped propagate the myth of a wholesome age of chivalry populated by courageous knights and damsels in distress. Medieval motifs were widely used in all the arts during the nineteenth century and were still popular early this century when Royal Doulton introduced their *King Arthur's Knight's* and *Falconry* series.

Side by side with this Medievalism there was a thriving Georgian revival. The novels of Austen, Goldsmith, Dobson and others became popular again and their later Victorian illustrators visualised an idyllic world of stage coaches and sedan chairs, feasts and port wine, which Charles Noke re-interpreted for Series ware. Scenes of coaching inns crowded with beaming rustics quaffing merrily or with the local gentry meeting for the stirrup cup before the hunt, enjoyed enormous popularity well into the twentieth century.

Wiltshire Moonrakers.

The origin of this title is explained in a legend connected with the days of smuggling, when the excise officers were kept busy night and day in endeavouring to frustrate the designs of those who believed in free trade—at least in spirits. It appears that the scene was enacted "up north" near Devizes. A publican had engaged some yokels to bring home some smuggled kegs of brandy in a trap during the night and when nearing their destination the donkey bolted and the trap coming into collision with a bridge, was upset, the kegs of brandy rolling out into the stream underneath. Whilst trying to rescue the kegs with some hay rakes they found at hand, the cry of "Zisemin" was raised. Asking what they were about, one of the yokels told him they were raking for a cheese which had rolled into the water. At this the exciseman, laughing to see the yokels raking at the shadow of the moon rode off leaving the grinning countrymen at liberty to rescue the kegs of spirits and carry them off. Not so very soft, were they?

Postcard of 1918 featuring the story of the Wiltshire Moonrakers on which a popular Royal Doulton series was based.

A "Tally-Ho" Idyll, drawn by Hugh Thomson on which a number of hunting series were based.

The need to escape from reality has obviously not diminished this century. The painful memories of the Great War and the privations of the aftermath encouraged people to dream about life before when everything was greener or rosier in an unspoilt countryside. Charles Noke brought out many series to cater for this idyllic picture of rural England and struck a chord particularly with his advertising for the *Countryside* series which asked 'How many of our Sons of Empire in various climes look back to the villages of the Motherland, where a thatched cottage or a red-roofed farm will ever suggest "Home"'.

Tudor style cottages complete with oak beams, lattice windows and cosy inglenooks became for many the ideal home in the inter war years and it is not difficult to envisage many of the series in this book displayed on the homely Welsh dresser.

In contrast, at the same time, there was an interest in fashionable taste of earlier periods, particularly the Georgian era. Enthusiasts collected Sheraton and Hepplewhite furniture, mezzotints of famous paintings and revived the art of silhouette which had been very much in vogue during the eighteenth century. It was for this market that Charles Noke introduced the series based on Bartolozzi engravings and the various subjects in silhouette.

It was obviously not easy to wean public taste away from Olde Worlde imagery but occasionally the modern world does creep in, for instance in the *Surfers* series which reflects the sunbathing craze of the early 1920's. For the most part, however, Charles Noke was as content as his public to find his inspiration in times gone by. Browsing through periodicals he found several artists in sympathy with his ideas, such as Hugh Thomson, Charles Crombie and Victor Venner and their original drawings were developed into a number of popular series. Noke himself became expert at assimilating the graphic styles of his contemporaries. Many of the early Series ware designs were drawn by him and bear his facsimile signature. Rarely were other artists credited on the ware although a large team worked on the etchings and lithographs which were used.

Leonard Langley supervised this team until 1916 and his initials were used in a numbering system for early patterns. George Holdcroft worked as an etcher at Royal Doulton for over sixty-seven years and gained the reputation of being one of the finest etchers in the Potteries. Many series must have flowed from his pen but only one is on record as his design, the desirable *Early Motoring* series. Another artist with outstanding long service was Walter Grace, who was associated with Series wares for over fifty years, interpreting Noke's ideas and developing his own such as *Old English Coaching Scenes* and *Home Waters* both of which are signed. The only other artist privileged to sign his work appears to have been Walter Nunn who designed some of the early series for example *An Old Jarvey.*

An even larger team of craftsmen were kept busy applying these artists' prints to the earthenware and occasionally bone china shapes, often colouring them by hand and dipping them in the various glazes used, such as the standard ivory or the more unusual golden yellow Holbein effect.

The Second World War interrupted this thriving aspect of Royal Doulton's business and it is only in the last decade that decorative plates have become very fashionable again. Nostalgia still reigns strong as is apparent in two of Royal Doulton's recent plate series celebrating Valentine's Day and Christmas.

For collectors with a romantic frame of mind, there will be plenty of interest in this book. It would be possible to assemble a most attractive collection of plates from these pages or to endeavour to trace every scene and shape in a particular series. This would be a daunting task in the case of the *Night Watchman* series for instance, which boasts twenty-six different characters but then that is the joy of collecting and the reason Charles Noke invented Series ware.

Catalogue pages featuring *Countryside* and *Coaching Days*, two of the most popular series.

Top to bottom, left to right Egyptian Pottery jug, New Cavaliers jug, Early Motoring jug, Gleaners teapot, The Toast jug, Cotswold Shepherd coffee pot, Welsh jug, Gaffers jug, Old English Country Fairs stein, Toasting Mottoes jug, Isle of Man vase, Nightwatchman jug, Skating vase, New Cavaliers stein, Jesters jug, Golf jug, Isle of Man vase, King Arthur's Knights jug.

How to use this book

The series in this volume are divided into six sections: In a Man's World; Feminine Society; Travel through the Ages; Life on the Ocean Wave; Rural England; Sports and Leisure. Each series is listed alphabetically within the section under its correct title if known, otherwise its most common title. When the exact title is not known, the series can be located with reference to the index which lists names of characters featured or quotations and inscriptions.

After some brief introductory remarks on the subject matter covered in each section, the information on each series is entered under several headings for easy reference.

SCENES/TITLES

In each series the number of different scenes depicted can range from one to around twenty. When the exact title of the scene has been recorded, quotation marks are used. Otherwise a description of the image is given to aid identification.

CHARACTERS

Some series such as *Night Watchman* have this additional heading where all the different figure poses recorded in that series are described.

PATTERN NUMBERS

All the D or E numbers so far recorded for each series are listed together. Sometimes one pattern number can refer to the entire series, for example D5561 is the *Cotswold Shepherd* series. In this case the pattern number can be a useful aid for tracing more items in the series. More often, however, each series has several different pattern numbers which denote the use of varying colourways, borders or shapes. The date of introduction of each design is indicated by the pattern number. See the *Date Guide* on page 141.

BORDERS

When a pattern was produced with more than one border, the variations are listed under this heading. For example, *Skaters* has four borders so far recorded: Greek key, wavy line, stylised leaves and skaters. Whenever possible border variants have been illustrated.

COLOURWAYS

The majority of Doulton series ware decoration is polychrome and in this case no specific reference is made to colour. However, any other variations are listed such as blue and white, sepia, or green and white. When unusual glaze effects or bodies are recorded these are also listed, for example Holbein glaze, a rich yellow effect; Whieldon ware, a rather coarse earthenware, or Celadon ware, glazed a subtle green.

SHAPES

An enormous variety of shapes were used in the series ware range. Under this heading an indication is given of the extent of each series and the types of shapes employed for that pattern. By consulting the *Shape Guide* in Volume One, collectors may become familiar with the most common vase numbers and shape names. Many items are not illustrated in the shape guide, in particular the diverse bone china shapes and specially moulded items.

DATES

The introduction and withdrawal dates are given when they are recorded. Pattern numbers are a useful guide to dating in conjunction with the *Pattern and Code Numbers Guide (Date Guide)* on page 141.

DESIGNER

The designer's name is given when it is known, but this is rarely the case.

SPECIAL BACKSTAMP

In addition to the Royal Doulton trademark some series had their own specially designed backstamp. Examples of some of the more interesting are given below.

The information for this book has been gleaned from surviving Doulton pattern books and from major collections. Although this is the most comprehensive study on Series ware produced so far it cannot claim to be complete. Some of Doulton's records are missing and with them, no doubt, further details of Series ware scenes, pattern numbers, glaze effects and so on. It is hoped that collectors will inform us of any additional material they discover in order that future studies will be more complete.

A selection of illustrated backstamps.

Rack plates, *top to bottom, left to right* Professionals, The Nineteenth Hole, Portraits, Monks and Mottoes, The Coaching Party, Teatime Sayings, Gallant Fishers, Wiltshire Moonrakers, Market Day A, Dutch, Chivalry, Golf

In a Man's World

This section, featuring aspects of Britain's colourful history, shows quite clearly to what extent the past has been 'A Man's World'.

In Medieval times the king and his court would travel from one castle to another during the year to administer justice and to maintain control of all parts of the realm. Such a visit was the focal point for all the nobles in that region to meet, often for a tournament which served a useful purpose by keeping military skills to the fore during peacetime. Afterwards the lords and ladies would be entertained by jesters, more commonly called fools, and by minstrels or troubadours. Although the wealthiest houses would have permanent musicians the role of the minstrel was important for, as they travelled around the country with harp or lute, they would give news of major events happening elsewhere and would also be well-versed in the epic stories of the past.

Art and literature were the domain of the church, and in particular of the monasteries, often under the patronage of some great noble. The monks were usually the only people in an area who could read and write. Many monastic communities were great landowners and their Abbots were leading figures in secular as well as religious affairs. Being largely self-sufficient they kept their own cellars, usually very well stocked, such as that attributed to Simon the Cellarer who reputedly kept a 'rare stock of Malmsey and Malvoisie'. It is no wonder that some monasteries were better known for their rowdiness than their godliness!

The Tudor and Stuart reigns saw the transition from a military to a civilian role for the nobility despite the disruption of the civil war which pitted Cavaliers against Roundheads. The gaiety of the Jacobean era was revived during the Restoration and Charles II became known as The Merry Monarch. In this relaxed period, homes were built without fortifications and more scholarly occupations were pursued. Every gentleman had his library and younger sons were encouraged to become parsons and doctors if they chose not to enter the army or navy. Such professional men, together with the squire, formed the nucleus of country society.

Towns flourished as never before; the mayor was usually drawn from the wealthy merchant class and before there was a police-force, nightwatchmen guarded against footpads. For many years the latest news was proclaimed by the town crier, until a more literate society gave rise to newspapers.

Jacobean

SCENES/TITLES
1 'Ye Little Bottel'. Cavalier standing right, another behind table and another lolling in front
2 'Ye Old Crown and Sceptre'. Cavalier reading to another seated holding tankard and another also seated at table
3 'Ye Old Belle'. Serving wench bringing drinks to two cavaliers

PATTERN NUMBERS
D837, D913, D1011, D1037, D1097, D1128, D1462, D1465

BORDERS
Pub signs

COLOURWAYS
Polychrome, blue and white, Whieldon, Holbein

SHAPES
Dundee jug, jug B, Breda teaset, Ball teaset

DATES
This series was introduced in 1901. The date of withdrawal is not recorded although it would have been before 1936.

SPECIAL BACKSTAMP

Notes Scene 1 is also found with song inscribed: 'The good young man that died'. Scene 2 is also found with mottoes: (a) 'Kissing goes by favour but when the kiss is stolen bliss the sweeter is the flavour'. (b) 'O Burton Ale it sparkles so prettily it makes us keep singing and rhyming so wittily. Not all the slip slops from your France, Spain and Italy can equal for poets our good Burton Ale'.

Jacobean. Jug 2.

Jacobean. *Above* 2, *centre* 1, *below* 3, border motifs.

Jesters

SCENES/TITLES
1 'Come and Welcome – Pass by and no offence'
2 'Many kiss the child for the nurse's sake'
3 'Penny in pocket is a merry companion'

CHARACTERS
1 Smiling jester
2 Laughing jester
3 Winking jester

PATTERN NUMBERS
D2537

BORDERS
Bells

COLOURWAYS
Polychrome

SHAPES
Herrick jug, Bisley jug

DATES
This series was introduced in 1906. The date of withdrawal is not recorded although it would have been before 1936.

DESIGNER
C J Noke

Jesters. Jug 1, bells border.

Jesters. 3.

Jesters. 2.

King Arthur's Knights or Tournament

SCENES/TITLES
1 Two knights, the one in the foreground on a rearing horse, the other with his lance over his shoulder
2 Rear view knight
3 Two knights, the one in foreground with lance, the other with lance over shoulder and shield
4 Knight with dragon slain
5 Two knights, the one in the background on rearing horse
6 Two knights, the one in the foreground with a lion rampant on his shield
7 Two knights, the one in the background holding his lance vertically
8 Solitary knight trotting
9 Two knights with page
10 Two knights galloping with lances horizontal
11 Two knights galloping with lances vertical
12 Solitary knight stationary

PATTERN NUMBERS
D2961, D3120

BORDERS
Laurel leaf, foliate scroll

COLOURWAYS
Polychrome, celadon

SHAPES
Teapot A and matching jug, match striker, stein

DATES
This series was introduced in 1908 and withdrawn by 1930.

King Arthur's Knights. Rack plates and jug, *left to right* 1, 2, 3, laurel leaf border.

King Arthur's Knights. *Left to right, above* 1, 5, *below* 6, 7.

King Arthur's Knights.
Jug 4, foliate scroll
border.

King Arthur's Knights.
Top to bottom 8, 10, 9, 11.

King Arthur's Knights. Matchstriker 12.

Minstrels

CHARACTERS
1 Profile minstrel playing recorder
2 Minstrel carrying lantern
3 Minstrel playing gong
4 Minstrel singing
5 Minstrel playing lute
6 Front view of minstrel playing recorder

PATTERN NUMBERS
D4243

BORDERS
Ribbons and lanterns

COLOURWAYS
Polychrome

SHAPES
Octagonal rack plate, Octagon teaset, Virginia tobacco jar, Octagon salad bowl, Rex mug, Pelican candlesticks

DATES
This series was introduced in 1923 and withdrawn by 1940.

15

Minstrels. Jug, *left to right* 2, 3, 1, ribbons and lantern border.

Minstrels. Jug, *left to right*, 4, 5, 6.

Monks A
SCENES/TITLES
1 Eating the boar's head

PATTERN NUMBERS
Not recorded

SHAPES
Not recorded

DATES
This scene appears in a pattern book of c1915.

Monks B
CHARACTERS
1 Monk with arms behind back
2 Monk with cane
3 Monk with bible under his arm
4 Monk reading the bible and looking up
5 Monk turning over the pages of a bible
6 Monk with his arms clasped in front

PATTERN NUMBERS
D2536

BORDERS
Bells

COLOURWAYS
Polychrome

SHAPES
Hecla jug

DATES
This series was introduced in 1906 and withdrawn by 1919.

Monks. A1.

Monks. Jug *left to right* B3, B2, B1.

16

Monks C

CHARACTERS
1 Head of monk drinking from a bottle
2 Head of monk reading
3 Profile head of monk wearing an apron
4 Profile head of monk with deep cowl facing right
5 Profile head of monk with deep cowl facing left
6 Front view of head of monk wearing apron and cap
7 Front view of head of monk wearing apron
8 Full figure monk with hands in sleeves

PATTERN NUMBERS
D2385

COLOURWAYS
Whieldon

SHAPES
Friar cream jug

DATES
This series was introduced in 1906 and withdrawn by 1919.

Notes This series is an adaptation of *Monks in the Cellar* and occasionally the two series are combined on one item.

Monks. *Left to right* B5, B4, B6.

Monks. *Left to right, above* C5, C6, C7, C8, *centre* C5, C1, C2, *below* C3, C4, C6, C1.

Monks and Mottoes A

SCENES/TITLES
1 'Tomorrow will be Friday'

CHARACTERS
1 A monk fishing

PATTERN NUMBERS
D3429

COLOURWAYS
Polychrome

SHAPES
Rack plate

DATES
This series was introduced in 1911 and withdrawn by 1928.

DESIGNER
C J Noke

Monks and Mottoes. Rack plate, A1.

17

Monks and Mottoes.
Rack plates, *left to right* B2,
B1, stylised leaf border.

Monks and Mottoes B
SCENES/TITLES
1 'A merry heart is a purse well lined'
2 'A contented mind is a blessing kind'

CHARACTERS
1 Monk (appears with scene 1 above)
2 Bishop (appears with scene 2 above)

PATTERN NUMBERS
D3571, D3661

BORDERS
Stylised leaf

COLOURWAYS
Blue, yellow and green, yellow and maroon,
brown and gold

SHAPES
Rack plates

DATES
This series was introduced in 1912 and
withdrawn by 1928

Monks and Mottoes C
SCENES/TITLES
1 'So farther and fare worse'

CHARACTERS
1 Monk having tea with two ladies

PATTERN NUMBERS
D3510, D3574, D3575

COLOURWAYS
Polychrome, sepia, Whieldon

SHAPES
Ball teapot

DATES
This series was introduced in 1912 and
withdrawn by 1928

Monks and Mottoes. C1.

Monks in the Cellar
SCENES/TITLES
1 Monk inspecting fish accompanied by cook
2 Monk drinking from a bottle, carrying a
basket of bottles
3 Grumpy monk with hands on hips
4 Monk leaning on barrel, glass raised
5 Monk with hands on hips looking at ground
6 Monk with hands on hips

PATTERN NUMBERS
D2385, D2567, D2877, D2976, D6099

BORDERS
Scallop shell and scroll

COLOURWAYS
Polychrome, Whieldon, Holbein, sepia and
green

SHAPES
Rack plate, Friar teapot, Friar jug, stein, chop
plate, Becket jug, round salad bowl

Monks in the Cellar. Rack plates, *left to right* 1, 5.

Monks in the Cellar. Rack plates and jug, *left to right* 4, 2, 6

DATES
This series was introduced in 1906, a chop plate was added to the range of shapes in 1939. The date of withdrawl is not recorded.

DESIGNER
C J Noke

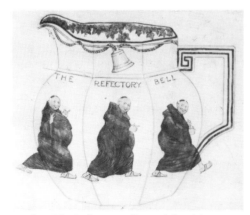

Monks – The Refectory Bell. Jug, *left to right* 3, 2, 1, bells border.

Monks – The Refectory Bell
CHARACTERS
1 Monk with thumbs up
2 Monk pointing
3 Monk holding lapels
4 Monk with both hands out
5 Monk with hands behind back
6 Monk with hands on hips
7 Monk with hands out, left foot in air
8 Monk with both arms raised up
9 Monk leaning back both arms in front, right foot in air
10 Monk with both arms raised, right leg kicked high
11 Monk striding, right hand pointing down

PATTERN NUMBERS
D2536, D3608

BORDERS
Bells

COLOURWAYS
Polychrome

SHAPES
Rack plate, Hecla jug, Octagon bowl

DATES
This series was introduced in 1906 and withdrawn by 1930

19

Monks – The Refectory Bell. *Left to right, above* 4, 3, 7, 2 *below* 6, 9, 8, 11, 10, 5.

New Cavaliers

SCENES/TITLES
1 'Ever drink, ever dry'
2 'Better so than worse'
3 'Better do it than wish it done'

Notes These mottoes are occasionally found in association with the characters below

New Cavaliers. *Above* 6 & 10, *below* 4 and titles 1 and 2.

New Cavaliers. Steins and jug, *left to right* 10, 2, 3.

New Cavaliers. Jug, *left to right* 1 & 2.

CHARACTERS
1 Three-quarter view cavalier, sword in left hand, glass in right
2 Front view cavalier, left hand on hip, right hand holding glass
3 Two cavaliers playing dice
4 Cavalier with elbow on table
5 Cavaliers with arms outstretched
6 Cavalier leaning on chair
7 Three-quarter view cavalier, maltese cross on cape
8 Front view cavalier, left hand on hip with sword, right hand holding glass
9 Cavalier standing with arms behind back
10 Cavalier leaning in doorway

PATTERN NUMBERS
D2875, D2966, D3051, D4006, D4749, D5105

New Cavaliers. Rack plates, *left to right* 5 & 9, 1 & 8, 7 & 9, lion and shield border.

BORDERS
Scroll and shell, lion and shield

COLOURWAYS
Polychrome

SHAPES
Rack plate, Clent jug, teapot A, Lennox flower bowl, York sandwich tray, round salad bowl, stein, Teniers jug, jug 7040B

DATES
This series was introduced in 1907 and extended until 1931. The date of withdrawal is not recorded

Notes The stein was adopted for advertising Teofani cigarettes

Nightwatchman
CHARACTERS
1 Front view, lantern in left hand, pipe in right
2 Front view with pike and lantern vertical in left hand, stick in right
3 Front view, reading with pike in right hand
4 Front view, pike and lantern over left shoulder, stick in right hand
5 Front view with pike in left hand, lantern in right
6 Front view, stick in right hand, lantern in left
7 Front view, resting cane on bollard
8 Front view, shaking left fist, pike in right hand

9 Three-quarter view fat watchman, pike over right shoulder, lantern in left hand
10 Three-quarter back view, pike over left shoulder, lantern in right hand
11 Three-quarter back view, pike and lantern over left shoulder, stick in right hand
12 Three-quarter view, pike in left hand, lantern in right
13 Three-quarter view, stick in right hand, lantern in left hand
14 Three-quarter view, pike over right shoulder, lantern in left
15 Three-quarter view, pike over left shoulder, lantern in right
16 Three-quarter view, pike and lantern over right shoulder, stick in left
17 Profile view thin watchman, pike over right shoulder, lantern in left hand
18 Profile view, pike over right shoulder, lantern in left hand
19 Profile view, stick in left hand, lantern in right
20 Profile view, stick in left hand, lantern in right, no pocket on coat
21 Profile view, pike over left shoulder, lantern in right hand, tiered cape on coat
22 Profile view, pike and lantern over right shoulder
23 Profile view, pike over left shoulder, lantern in right hand
24 Profile view, pike under right arm, lantern in left hand
25 Two watchmen talking, one with pike over right shoulder, the other, lantern in left hand, stick in right
26 Two watchmen talking, one rear view, pike

Night Watchman. Rack plates, *left to right* 8, 24, 3.

Night Watchman. Jugs, *left to right* 7, 11, 18, 2, Swag and fruit, flower and foliate scroll borders.

Night Watchman. Jugs, *left to right* 10, 19, 4, 9, Morris flowers and vertical stripes borders.

in right hand, the other front view, lantern in right hand
27 Two watchmen talking, one with stick and lantern, the other with pike and stick

PATTERN NUMBERS
D159, D1086, D1198, D1200, D1231, D1232, D1233, D1336, D1454, D1456, D1457, D1458, D1459, D1460, D1491, D1498, D1499, D1500, D1511, D1788, D1833, D1885, D1887, D1891, D1907, D1909, D1910, D1940, D1944, D1984, D1997, D2002, D2107, D2127, D2134, D2372, D2422, D2747, D3190, D4746, D5478

BORDERS
Morris flowers, swag and fruit, vertical stripes, foliate scroll, gilt branches, shell and lace, fuchsia, gilt flowers

COLOURWAYS
Whieldon, blue and white

SHAPES
Baron, Teniers, Tavern, Tudor, Clent, Armada,

Castle and Breda jugs, Breda teapot, Ceylon teaset, unrecorded spittoon, unrecorded jug, ice jug, Lennox bowl, unrecorded toilet set, jug 7119, candlestick 7277, jug B, Pelican trinket set, Regent bowl, Flagon toilet set, Leeds fruit dish, Vase numbers 7018, 7493

DATES
This series was introduced in 1899 and extended until 1935. It was withdrawn by 1945

DESIGNER
C J Noke

Notes Some items are found with quotation 'Watchman, what of the night?' Motto sometimes found on Flagon jug 'Those who have money are troubled about it those who have none are troubled without it'. Motto sometimes found on Tavern jug 'Full many a shaft at random sent finds mark the archer little meant and many a word at random spoken. can wound or heal a heart that's broken'.

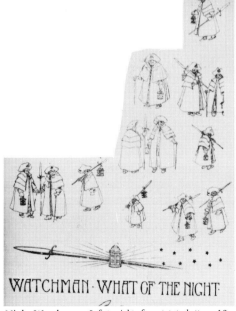

Night Watchman. *Left to right, from top to bottom*, 12, 6, 25, 26, 21, 27, 22, 16, 14, 23.

Night Watchman, *left to right, above*, 10, 9, 1, 10, *centre* 5, 17, 4, 15, 11, *below* 19, 11, 19, 20, 2.

Old English Scenes, Rack plates, *from top to bottom* 4, 2, 1, 3.

Old English Scenes

SCENES/TITLES
1 'The broom man maketh his living most sweet'
2 'Roger Solemel Cobbler'
3 'Where broken gamesters oft repair their loss'
4 'The justice's late meeting'

PATTERN NUMBERS
D4729, D4832, D4833, D4834, D4835, D6302

COLOURWAYS
Polychrome

SHAPES
Rack plate

DATES
This series was introduced in 1927 and was withdrawn in 1942. However, *Roger Solemel Cobbler* was reissued alone in 1949 and would have been withdrawn by 1967

DESIGNER
After drawings by Hugh Thomson which featured in the English Illustrated Magazine of 1889 as illustrations to *Who liveth so merry* by Deutoromelia and *A journey to Exeter* by John Gay.

Professionals

SCENES/TITLES
1 'The Falconer'
2 'The Admiral'
3 'The Parson'
4 'The Hunting Man'
5 'The Squire'
6 'The Doctor'
7 'The Bookworm'
8 'The Mayor'
9 'The Jester'

PATTERN NUMBERS
D3080, D3089, D3117, D3189, D3303, D3348, D3349, D3616, D3684, D3756, D3930, D3931, D3932, D3933, D5898, D5899, D5901, D5902, D5903, D5904, D5905, D5906, D5907, D6277, D6278, D6279, D6280, D6281, D6282, D6283, D6284, TC1044, TC1045, TC1046, TC1047, TC1048, TC1049, TC1050, TC1051

BORDERS
Library, shelf of bottles and bowls, riding crop and bugle, trophies and scrolls, flying birds, lanterns, ships, loop

Professionals. Rack plates, *from left to right, above*, 1, 2, 3, *centre*, 4, 5, 6, *below*, 7, 8, 9.

COLOURWAYS
Polychrome

SHAPES
Rack plates

DATES
This series was introduced in 1909. Slight modifications were made in 1915, 1938 and 1948 when the series was renumbered. An English translucent version was introduced in 1968. The series was withdrawn in 1975. The Bookworm was only made between 1909 and 1949.

Should Auld Acquaintance Be Forgot

SCENES/TITLES
1 Party of one-legged men

PATTERN NUMBERS
D2556, D2607, D4575

BORDERS
Stylised leaves

COLOURWAYS
Polychrome, blue and green, Whieldon

SHAPES
Rack plate, tobacco jar

DATES
This series was introduced in 1906 and
extended in 1926. The date of withdrawal is not
recorded although it was probably by World
War II.

Notes The following quotation is found on the
tobacco jar: 'He who will calmly smoke will
think like a sage and act like a samaritan'.

Should Auld Acquaintance Be Forgot, Rack
plate, 1.

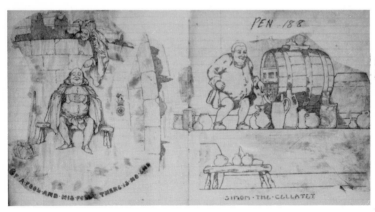

Simon the Cellarer.
Left to right 2, 1.

Simon the Cellarer

SCENES/TITLES
1 'Simon, the Cellarer'
2 'Of a Fool and his folly there is no end'

CHARACTERS
1 Simon the Cellarer tapping the barrel
  (appears on scene 1 above)
2 Jester tickling sleeping man's nose (appears
  on scene 2 above)

PATTERN NUMBERS
D3972

COLOURWAYS
Polychrome

SHAPES
Rack plate, Tudor jug

DATES
This series was introduced in 1916. The date of
withdrawal is not recorded although it would
have been before 1936.

The Stirrup Cup. Rack plates, *left to right* 1, 2, scallop scroll border.

The Stirrup Cup

SCENES/TITLES
1 'The Stirrup Cup'
2 'Speed the Parting Guest'
3 'Here's a Health unto his Majesty'

CHARACTERS
1 Cavalier with hand on hip and glass in hand
   facing serving wench
2 Cavalier with glass being served by monks
3 Cavalier toasting

PATTERN NUMBERS
D3045, D3046, D3084, D3568

BORDERS
Scallop scroll, reversed V

COLOURWAYS
Polychrome, blue and white, sepia

SHAPES
Rack plate, Tavern jug, Tudor jug

DATES
This series was introduced in 1908 and
withdrawn by 1929

The Stirrup Cup. Jug, 3, reversed V border.

The Toast

SCENES/TITLES
1 'For he's a jolly good fellow which nobody
  can deny'

CHARACTERS
1 Two men in eighteenth century dress toasting
  seated man

PATTERN NUMBERS
D3971

COLOURWAYS
Polychrome

SHAPES
Tudor jug

DATES
This series was introduced in 1916. The date of
withdrawal is not recorded although it would
have been before 1936.

The Toast. Jug 1.

Toasting Mottoes A

SCENES/TITLES
1 'Here's to the man who is pleased with his lot
  And never sits sighing for what he has not'
2 'It is hard for an empty bag to stand upright'
3 Motto not recorded

CHARACTERS
1 White haired man with punch bowl and
  audience
2 Bald man and audience
3 Man in dark wig and audience

PATTERN NUMBERS
D1573

COLOURWAYS
Blue and white with red

SHAPES
Tavern jug (two sizes)

DATES
This series was introduced in 1903. The date of
withdrawal is not recorded although it would
have been before 1936

DESIGNER
C J Noke

Toasting Mottoes, A3.

Toasting Mottoes.
Jugs, *left to right* A2, A1.

Toasting Mottoes B
SCENES/TITLES
1 'An open door may tempt a saint'

CHARACTERS
1 Two cavaliers drinking and smoking

PATTERN NUMBERS
D3427

COLOURWAYS
Polychrome

SHAPES
Rack plate

DATES
This series was introduced in 1914 and
withdrawn by 1929

Toasting Mottoes. Rack plate B1.

Toasting Scenes
SCENES/TITLES
1 'Our Noble Selves'
2 'Sweethearts and Wives'
3 'The King God bless him'

CHARACTERS
1 Seated gentleman in hat with standing
  gentleman wearing sword, both toasting
2 Two bearded gentlemen side by side raising
  glasses
3 Gentleman on his own with raised glass

PATTERN NUMBERS
Not recorded

SHAPES
Not recorded

DATES
This series appears in a pattern book of c1902

Toasting Scenes. *Above* 2, *centre* 1,
below 3.

Town Officials. Rack plates, *left to right* 3, 1, 2.

Town Officials
SCENES/TITLES
1 Town crier ringing bell
2 Town crier making announcement
3 Night watchman with pike and lantern in
front of stocks

PATTERN NUMBERS
D2716, D3682

COLOURWAYS
Polychrome

SHAPES
Rack plates, Tudor jug

DATES
This series was introduced in 1906 and added
to in 1913. It was withdrawn by 1941

Notes The quotation: 'He is rich who craves
nothing' is sometimes found on scene 3

Feminine Society

Society was dominated by men in the Middle Ages and women were very restricted in the lives they could lead. It was the Age of Chivalry, both in fact with the Crusades, and in fiction with the popularity of romances such as Sir Thomas Malory's Morte d'Arthur, in which women were protected, fêted and honoured.

From Elizabethan times women had more freedom and joined more fully into society, often exerting great influence behind the scenes. In the seventeenth century, fashionable ladies held salons in their homes where they entertained leading figures, such as politicians, artists and playwrights. These gatherings continued throughout the Georgian era and the decor of the salon itself was continually updated to reflect the latest mode. In the neo-classical period, the wealthy hung their walls with large allegorical paintings, the less affluent with the latest engravings by Bartolozzi.

Many social exchanges took place outdoors, either in the carefully landscaped parks of Capability Brown or in the formal Italian gardens with their shrubs cut into complicated forms – the art of topiary. To protect their dresses ladies rode in sedan-chairs, rather than walk short distances.

In Regency London both men and women strolled, rode or were driven down Rotten Row, in Hyde Park, to see and be seen. Later Kensington Gardens became another fashionable place to take the air, and it is still a favourite haunt of the redoubtable British Nanny for the daily walk before tea. Afternoon tea is a national institution, enjoyed in every home in the country, from the smallest cottage to Buckingham Palace.

A Hundred Years Ago

SCENES/TITLES

1 Family at tea, father with arms folded resting on cane
2 Family at tea, with one child, father on right smoking
3 Family at tea, with one child, father on left with raised cup
4 Family drinking tea, with two children, father on right
5 Family drinking tea, with one child, father on left
6 Family at tea, with two children, father on left smoking
7 Husband and wife at tea, he is smoking
8 Man seated in garden amongst flowers
9 Husband and wife at tea, he is holding his pipe and gesticulating
10 Husband and wife at tea, he has pipe in one hand, teacup in other
11 Couple having tea, husband smoking in front of table, wife drinking tea behind

PATTERN NUMBERS
D3794, D5499

COLOURWAYS
Polychrome

SHAPES
Rack plate, Quorn teaset, Joan teapot, shaped tea plates, fruit plates, cup and saucer

DATES
This series was introduced in 1934 and withdrawn by 1946

Notes The Joan teapot is found featuring Scene 11 and inscribed 'After fifty years'.

A Hundred Years Ago. 11.

A Hundred Years Ago.
Left to right, above, 3, 4, *below* 5.

A Hundred Years Ago.
Left to right, above, 6, 10, 7, *below* 8, 9.

A Hundred Years Ago. Rack plates, *left to right* 1, 2.

Bartolozzi Etchings

SCENES/TITLES
1 Horace
2 Rinalda and Armida
3 The Judgement of Paris
4 Zeuxis composing the picture of Juno
5 Griselda
6 Cupids 1
7 Cupids 2
8 Venus surrounded by cupids
9 Two ladies and cupid with bird

PATTERN NUMBERS
D3024, D4847, D4848, D5054, D5055

COLOURWAYS
Sepia

SHAPES
Rack plates

DATES
This series was introduced in 1929. The date of withdrawal is not recorded

Notes These designs are taken from etchings by Bartolozzi after paintings by Angelica Kauffman (numbers 1–5), Lady Diana Beauclerk (numbers 6 and 7) and B Cipriani (number 8)

Bartolozzi. Rack Plate 2.

Bartolozzi. *Left to right* 8, 3, 6.

Bartolozzi. *Left to right* 5, 4.

Bartolozzi. *Left to right* 7, 1, 9.

Chivalry. *Left to right*, 3, 4.

Chivalry. *Above* incidental border, *below* 5.

Chivalry 6.

Chivalry

SCENES/TITLES
1 Two ladies seated with a peacock
2 Lady being crowned with floral wreath, gentleman playing lute
3 Lady with doves and rabbits
4 Two ladies with a doe
5 Lady on horseback being led by page

6 Lady on horseback with page and lady walking dog meeting gentleman leading horse

PATTERN NUMBERS
D5030, D5158

BORDERS
Scene of lady and gentleman on horseback and page with dog

Chivalry. Rack Plates, *left to right* 1, 2.

COLOURWAYS
Polychrome

SHAPES
Rack plate, sandwich tray, square shaped teaplate

DATES
This series was introduced in 1930 and withdrawn by 1945

DESIGNER
W Nunn

SPECIAL BACKSTAMP

Edwardian Ladies. *Left to right* 3, 4.

Edwardian Ladies

SCENES/TITLES
1 Lady with basket of flowers
2 Lady with bird on elbow
3 Lady holding skirt with one hand
4 Lady holding skirt with two hands
5 Lady with hands clasped at neck
6 Lady beckoning to birds
7 Lady holding garland aloft
8 Lady holding rose branch aloft

PATTERN NUMBERS
D3200

BORDERS
Roses

COLOURWAYS
Polychrome

SHAPES
Rack plates

DATES
This series was introduced in 1909. The date of withdrawal is not recorded

Edwardian Ladies. Rack plate 6.

Edwardian Ladies 2.

Edwardian Ladies. *Left to right* 5, 1.

Edwardian Ladies. *Left to right,* 7, 8.

Eighteenth Century Garden Scenes
SCENES/TITLES
1 Two ladies sitting under tree, man standing
2 Man serenading lady with guitar
3 Man playing flute for two ladies
4 Youth sitting with two dogs

PATTERN NUMBERS
D3661

COLOURWAYS
Polychrome

SHAPES
Unrecorded jug

Eighteenth Century Garden Scenes. *Left to right, above* 4, 1, *below* 3, 2.

DATES
This series was introduced in 1913. The date of withdrawal is not recorded although it would have been before 1936

37

Kensington Gardens

SCENES/TITLES
1 Horsemen with dogs
2 Carriage with pedestrian following
3 Three horsemen with dogs, one waving
4 Single horseman with two pedestrians and two dogs
5 Two horsemen and lady
6 Scattered horsemen and dogs

PATTERN NUMBERS
D4467

BORDERS
Stylised leaves and flowers

COLOURWAYS
Polychrome

SHAPES
Rack plates, Quorn teaset, teapot stand, York sandwich tray, vase 7764, porridge plate, Virginia tobacco jar, salad bowl, oatmeal saucer, Craig and Ancester ashtrays, Leeds oval fruit dish, fruit saucer

DATES
This series was introduced in 1924 and withdrawn by 1942

Kensington Gardens.
Left 2, *above* 2, *below* 5.

Kensington Gardens. Vase 1.

Kensington Gardens. 4.

Medieval. *Left to right* 1, 5.

Kensington Gardens. Catalogue page Jug 24, features 6, Plate 5 inches features 3.

Medieval. 2.

Medieval

SCENES/TITLES
1 Gentleman with two ladies and laurel wreath
2 Lady playing lyre with two cherubs
3 Lady kneeling by her lyre
4 Gentleman and lady with flowers
5 Gentleman and lady with laurel wreath

PATTERN NUMBERS
D1775, D1828, D1830, D1831

BORDERS
Laurel leaf

COLOURWAYS
Blue and white, Whieldon

SHAPES
Umbrella stand, Regent bowl

DATES
This series was introduced in 1903 and withdrawn in 1919

Medieval. *Above* 4, *below* 3.

Old English Gardens. *Left to right, above 7, 11, 8, below* 10, 9, 2.

Old English Gardens. *Above* 1, *centre* 6, *below* 4.

Old English Gardens
SCENES/TITLES
1 Gentleman bowing to lady
2 Rear view of two ladies arm in arm
3 Rear view of two ladies with a man in background
4 Gentleman with two ladies seated on grass
5 Lady and gentleman walking past balustrade and garden sculpture
6 Lady and gentleman walking past balustrade
7 Lady with fan, gentleman with sash
8 Lady with dogs talking to two gentlemen
9 Lady holding skirts with cane
10 Fountain
11 Lady with fan and gentleman with cane

PATTERN NUMBERS
H3873, H3874

COLOURWAYS
Polychrome

DATES
This series features in a record book for 1929

Old English Gardens. *Above* 3, *below* 2.

Old English Sayings.
Rack plates, *left to
right* 2, 1.

Old English Sayings
SCENES/TITLES
1 'Joys shared with others are more than
enjoyed'
2 'A thing of beauty is a joy for ever'

PATTERN NUMBERS
D3458

BORDERS
Anthemion

COLOURWAYS
Polychrome, Holbein

SHAPES
Rack plates

DATES
This series was introduced in 1911 and
withdrawn by 1928

Notes The characters in this series are the same
as those in *Wedlock*

Portraits. Rack plate A1.

Portraits A
CHARACTERS
1 Portrait of a girl with long curly hair
2 Portrait of a girl in hat and scarf

PATTERN NUMBERS
Not recorded

BORDERS
Floral

COLOURWAYS
Sepia

Portraits. A2.

SHAPES
Rack plate

DATES
This series features in a record book of 1904

DESIGNER
J Ogden

Portraits. Rack plate B2.

Portraits B – Petra subjects

CHARACTERS
1 Front view of young girl with foliage
2 Profile view of young girl with foliage
3 Front view of girl with wispy hair
4 Three-quarter rear view of girl with hair up

PATTERN NUMBERS
D2883, D2884

BORDERS
Stylised leaves, anthemion and foliage

COLOURWAYS
Blue and white, Holbein

SHAPES
Rack plate

DATES
This series was introduced in 1907. The date of
withdrawal is not recorded although it would
have been before 1936

Portraits B4.

Portraits. *Left
to right* B1, B3.

Sedan Chair

CHARACTERS
1 Lady holding skirts in front of sedan chair with two attendants
2 Lady stepping out of sedan chair with three attendants
3 Two men carrying sedan chair

PATTERN NUMBERS
D3418, D3597

BORDERS
Topiary hedge

COLOURWAYS
Polychrome

SHAPES
Rack plate, Lennox flower bowl, Corinth teaset, Leeds round fruit dish

DATES
This series was introduced in 1912 and withdrawn by 1940

Notes Some items are found with the mottoes:
a 'Ask this purse what thou shouldst buy'
b 'As the wind blows so set your sail'

Sedan Chair. Rack plates, *left to right* 1, 3.

Sedan Chair 2.

Sundial 1.

Sundial

SCENES/TITLES
1 'With Warning Hand I mark time's rapid flight'

PATTERN NUMBERS
D3513

BORDER
Leaves

COLOURWAYS
Polychrome

SHAPES
Westcott jug, Joan teapot

DATES
This series was introduced in 1911. The date of withdrawal is not recorded although it would have been before 1936

Teatime Sayings A

SCENES/TITLES
1 'A good cup of tea. The cup that cheers'
2 'The best of men are only men at best'

CHARACTERS
1 Profile view old lady in ribboned cap drinking tea with little finger in air
2 Three-quarter view of old lady holding cup aloft
3 Profile view old lady drinking tea

PATTERN NUMBERS
D2667, D2799

BORDERS
Cups

COLOURWAYS
Polychrome, Whieldon

SHAPES
Ball teapot, Pekoe teapot, Royles self pouring
teapot, Clive teapot

DATES
This series was introduced in 1907 and
withdrawn by 1930

Teatime Sayings. *Above* character A3, *below*
character A2.

Teatime Sayings. Rack plate character
A1.

Teatime Sayings. B1.

Tea. *Left to right*
1, 2.

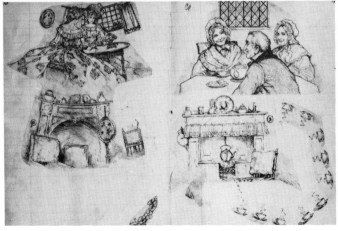

Teatime Sayings B
SCENES/TITLES
1 'Leave tomorrow till tomorrow'

CHARACTERS
1 Two old ladies having tea

PATTERN NUMBERS
D3977

COLOURWAYS
Polychrome

DATES
This design was introduced in 1916 and
withdrawn by 1930

Tea
SCENES/TITLES
1 Contrasting interiors

CHARACTERS
1 Two Victorian ladies of fashion taking tea
2 Two old ladies with man at tea

PATTERN NUMBERS
Not recorded

BORDER
Teacups

SHAPES
Not recorded

DATES
This series appears in a pattern book of 1915

Topiary
SCENES/TITLES
1 'Rest for the Weary' – a garden seat
2 'Welcome' – ornate garden

PATTERN NUMBERS
Not recorded

COLOURWAYS
Holbein

SHAPES
Corinth teapot, stein

DATES
This series features in a record book of 1913

Topiary. *Left to right* 2, 1.

Tudor Characters

CHARACTERS
1 Head of Tudor lady
2 Head of Tudor man
3 Tudor lady with lace bonnet

PATTERN NUMBERS
D3946, D3990, D3991

BORDERS
Scroll

COLOURWAYS
Polychrome

SHAPES
Rack plates

DATES
This series was introduced in 1916 and
withdrawn by 1932

Tudor Characters. Rack plate 1.

Tudor Characters. From *top to bottom* 2,
1, 3.

Valentine's Day and Christmas Annuals

Valentine's Day
SCENES/TITLES
First line of the verses on the back of each plate:
1976 'Many things must fade from view'
1977 'If all the world were forget-me-nots dear'
1978 'You'll ask me if I loved you?'
1979 'May time flow sweetly as a song'
1980 'How oft my bright and radiant eyes'
1981 'Tis true that thy accents which, present, I hear?'
1982 'To my fond love'
1983 'Dearest, wilt thou accept a heart'
1984 'Enshrined in my bosom'

BORDERS
Embossed with hearts and flowers

COLOURWAYS
Polychrome

SHAPES
Plates

DATES
This series was introduced in 1976 and a new design is issued annually

DESIGNER
Jo Ledger inspired by Victorian prints

SPECIAL BACKSTAMP

Christmas – First Collection
SCENES/TITLES
First line of the verses on the back of each plate
1977 'To friends, long parted, kindly greeting'
1978 'A merry Christmas, a life of joy'
1979 'All things bright be yours today'
1980 'Now thro' the land a welcome murmur steals'
1981 'O yes! A merrie Christmas'
1982 'When this happy tide'

BORDERS
Embossed with bells and holly

COLOURWAYS
Polychrome

SHAPES
Plates

DATES
This series was introduced in 1977 and a new design issued annually until 1982

DESIGNER
Jo Ledger inspired by Victorian prints

SPECIAL BACKSTAMP

Christmas – Second Collection
SCENES/TITLES
1 'Silent Night'	1983
2 'While Shepherds Watched'	1984
3 'O Little Town of Bethlehem'	
4 'We Saw Three Ships a Sailing'	
5 'The Holly and the Ivy'	
6 'Hark the Herald Angels Sing'	

BORDERS
Words and music from the featured carol

COLOURWAYS
Polychrome

SHAPES
Plates

DATES
This series was introduced in 1983. Scenes 3–6 will be assigned to the years 1985–1988

DESIGNER
Neil Faulkner

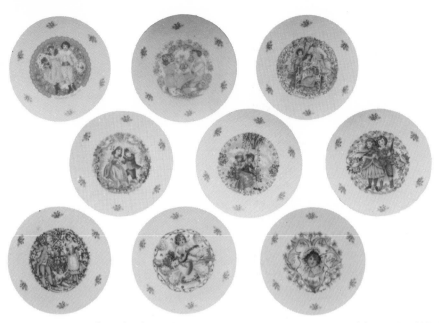

Valentine's Day. *Left to right, above* 1976, 1977, 1978, *centre* 1979, 1980, 1981, *below* 1982, 1983, 1984.

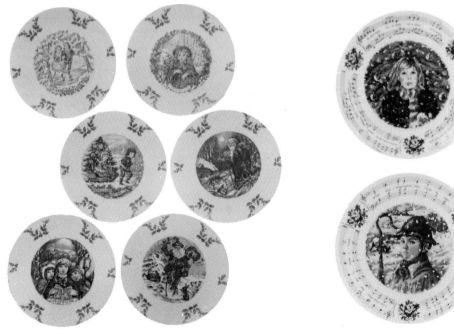

Christmas First Collection. *Left to right, above* 1977, 1978, *centre* 1979, 1980, *below* 1981, 1982.

Christmas Second Collection. *Above* 1983, *below* 1984.

Wedlock. *Left to right, above* 13, 12, 10, 14, 2, 6, 4, *below* 9, 3, 1, 7, 8, 11, 5.

Wedlock

SCENES/TITLES
1 'Wedlock's Joys do Sometimes change. Ho Merrily ho'
2 'Wedlock's Joys are Soft and Sweet. Ho Merrily ho'
3 'Wedlock is a Ticklish thing. Ho Merrily ho'

CHARACTERS
1 Lady with open parasol
2 Profile lady with open fan and cane
3 Profile lady gathering skirts and facing forward
4 Three-quarter view lady with skirts gathered over her arm
5 Three-quarter view lady holding her skirt in one hand and a fan in the other
6 Three-quarter view lady with one arm at her waist, the other holding an open fan
7 Lady with feathered headband holding closed fan
8 Three-quarter view gentleman leaning forward on his cane and holding his hat behind his back
9 Gentleman with one hand on his hip, the other on his cane
10 Gentleman holding top hat with other arm raised
11 Three-quarter view gentleman holding his top hat on his hip
12 Profile gentleman carrying cane
13 Gentleman holding hat in one hand, his other hand raised to his chest
14 Gentleman resting on his cane, his other hand held at his waist

PATTERN NUMBERS
D2395, D2477

Wedlock. Jug 2, 8.

BORDER
Grapes and vines border, diamond trellis and scroll

COLOURWAYS
Polychrome

SHAPES
Rack plates, Baron shape jug, Lennox flower bowl, Loving Cup 7342, Vase numbers 7023 and 7340

DATES
This series was introduced in 1905 and withdrawn by 1928

DESIGNER
J Ogden

49

Travel through the Ages

For hundreds of years travelling was a long, arduous business so many people never ventured further than their nearest market town. Not until the introduction of tolls in the mid seventeenth century did the roads improve and from that time horse travel expanded rapidly reaching a peak with the Regency era.

The poorest travellers sat on top of the slowest coaches while the more fortunate journeyed inside or by Royal Mail coach which raced dangerously fast as the drivers sought to establish new records and keep their lucrative mail franchises. For rich and poor alike there were frequent accidents and delays and highwaymen were always a threat. The coach drivers were great characters, heroes of small boys who dreamt of handling a team of horses as later generations dreamt of driving steam-engines. The hackney coach drivers were known as Jarveys, a corruption of the personal name Jervis. It is thought that the nick-name could derive from St. Gervase whose emblem was a whip. Their profession was threatened with the advent of the motor car. A source of wonder, the new noisy and disruptive machines were denounced at first as dangerous and dismissed as a passing fad. It was to be many years before they completely displaced the horse and carriage but now the roads belong to them.

An Old Jarvey

SCENES/TITLES
1 'An old jarvey'
2 'The coachman'

CHARACTERS
1 Front view coachman holding whip in two hands
2 Coachman with arms clasped, whip vertical in arm
3 Profile coachman with whip in left hand
4 Coachman discussing document
5 Front view coachman with whip vertical in left hand
6 Three-quarter view coachman with whip in right hand
7 Coachman with whip in left hand, coin in right

An Old Jarvey. Rack plate 5.

An Old Jarvey. *Left to right, above* 2, 3, *below* 1, 4.

An Old Jarvey. *Left to right* 2, 9, 10, 7, 10, 11.

8 Three-quarter view coachman with whip in left hand
9 Coachman with tankard of ale
10 Coachman with whip and suitcase
11 Coachman with whip in left hand holding the end of it in his right
12 Three quarter view coachman with whip in left hand

PATTERN NUMBERS
D3118, D4600, D5958

BORDERS
Coaches

COLOURWAYS
Whieldon

SHAPES
Tobacco jar, Loving Cup 7058, Tavern jug, round salad bowl

DATES
This series was introduced in 1909 and extended in 1926 and 1938. The date of withdrawal is not recorded

DESIGNER
W Nunn

An Old Jarvey. *Left to right, above* 12, 4, *centre* 9, 6, *below* 2, 7.

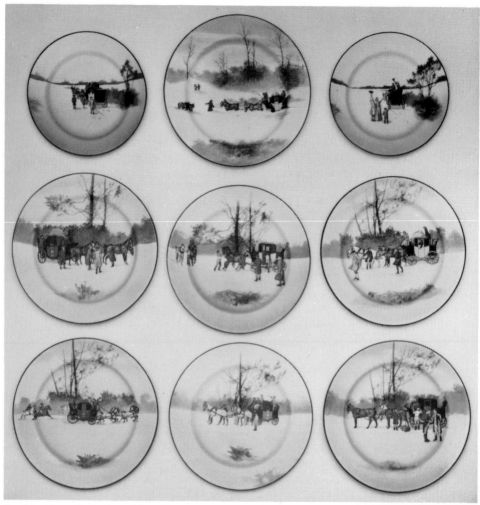

Coaching Days. Rack plates, *left to right, above* 12, 13, 8, *centre* 17, 1, 11, *below* 14, 6, 7.

Coaching Days
SCENES/TITLES

1 Coach being harnessed, attendant bringing up a pair of horses
2 Driver talking to serving wench
3 Youth holding a front pair of horses
4 Innkeeper talking to driver, attendants boarding
5 Group of passengers
6 Horn sounding, coach departing watched by solitary man

7 Driver talking to passenger, attendants loading
8 Family waving farewell
9 Man opening gate for the coach
10 Tightening the harness, goose and hare hanging from coach
11 Unscheduled stop, trouble with lame horses
12 Coach going up hill, attendants walking
13 Struggling through the snow, extra horses

14 Coach pursued by highwaymen
15 Boxes being handed to driver
16 Man with trunk, coach approaching through snow
17 Coach stopped, broken harness
18 Passenger sitting on a trunk, another beside
19 Group of passengers, horn sounding
20 Gig arriving with passenger

PATTERN NUMBERS
D2356, D2579, D2682, D2716, D3474, D4190, D4891, E2768, E3407, E3804, E5082, E5083

SHAPES
Earthenware. Rack plates, Ball teaset, Jubilee mug, Rex mug, Carlton bowls (two sizes), beaker, Rheims cup and saucer and cream, Pitt jug, teapot stand, porridge plate, oatmeal saucer, Octagon sweet, Astor celery tray, Leeds square, round and oval fruit dish, round salad bowl, Napier, Newrim, Ancester and 89 ashtrays, Lennox flower bowl, York sandwich tray, Pelican candlestick, Pomade box, puff box, vases numbers 7347, 7386, 7745, 8151, 8188, Mayfair toilet set
China. Rocket jug, Cecil plate, Stafford dessert, mug, Burke beaker, Cecil cup and saucer, Gwendoline sugar and cream, vases numbers 768, 850, 859, 1023, 1032A, 1058

DATES
This series was introduced in 1905, extended until 1929 and withdrawn in 1955

DESIGNER
Victor Venner (fl. 1904–24)

Coaching Days. *Left to right, above* 12, 3, 16, *centre* 4, 10, 9, *below* 8, 9, 20.

Coaching Days. Vase, dish and mugs. *Left to right* 16, 2, 18, 3.

Coaching Days. Catalogue page of bone china series. Scenes already illustrated except rim dish featuring 5 and mug featuring 19.

Coaching. New Edition. *Left to right* 6, 4.

Coaching (New edition)
SCENES/TITLES
1 'Ye Red Lion'
2 'Ye Black Lion'
3 Two yokels outside a coaching inn
4 Laden coach
5 Coachman
6 Old man with stick

PATTERN NUMBERS
Not recorded

COLOURWAYS
Polychrome

SHAPES
Not recorded

DATES
This series features in a pattern book of 1924

Coaching. New Edition. *Left to right, above* 3, 2,
below 5, 1.

The Coaching Party
SCENES/TITLES
1 'Old Bob Ye guard'
2 'William Ye Driver'
3 'Ye Squire, Ye Passenger'

PATTERN NUMBERS
D2645, D2698, D2723, D2724, D2809

BORDERS
Coaches and horses

COLOURWAYS
Polychrome and Whieldon

SHAPES
Rack plate, Tudor jug, Virginia tobacco jar, Jug
7119, Regent flower bowl

DATES
This series was introduced in 1906 and
withdrawn by 1928.

The Coaching Party. Rack plates, *left to right* 3, 1, 2.

Early Motoring. Rack plates, *left to right, above* 2, 7, 9, *below* 8, 1, 6.

Early Motoring. Jugs, *left to right* 3, 4, reverse of 3.

Early Motoring 5.

Early Motoring

SCENES/TITLES
1 'Blood Money'
2 'Deaf'
3 'A horse, a horse'
4 'After the Run'
5 'The New and the Old'
6 'A nerve tonic'
7 'Itch yer on guvnor'
8 'Room for One'
9 Yokel and motorist outside Chequers Inn

PATTERN NUMBRS

PATTERN NUMBERS
D2406, D3318

BORDERS
Landscape

COLOURWAYS
Polychrome

SHAPES
Simon jug, stein

DATES
This series was introduced in 1905 and
withdrawn by 1928

DESIGNER
G Holdcroft

Old English Coaching Scenes. Rack plates, *left to right* 5, 1, 2.

Old English Coaching Scenes. Plates, box and stein, *left to right* 6, 7, 4, 11, 3.

Old English Coaching
Scenes. 8.

Old English Coaching Scenes

SCENES/TITLES
1 The coach inside the coaching yard, loading
2 The coach driving through a village scattering chickens
3 A woman offering refreshments to the coach driver
4 A lady being helped out of the coach
5 The coach outside the Red Lion Inn, changing horses
6 The coach being waved off from a wayside inn
7 The coach moving slowly out of a village, watched by a man and his dog under a tree
8 Harnessing the horses and cleaning the coach observed by driver
9 The coach passing the Eagle Inn
10 The coach at the tollhouse
11 The coach galloping through a village
12 The coach coming through a village passing a lady with panniers of vegetables
13 A boy leading the horse
14 Coach galloping past a village watched by old man with dog

PATTERN NUMBERS
D6393

COLOURWAYS
Polychrome

SHAPES
Rack plate, square, oval and octagonal fruit dishes, salad bowl, comport, stein, cup and saucer, Avon chop dish, vases numbers: 8099, 7979, 8237, 7922 and 7923

DATES
This series was introduced in 1953 and withdrawn by 1967

DESIGNER
W E Grace

SPECIAL BACKSTAMP

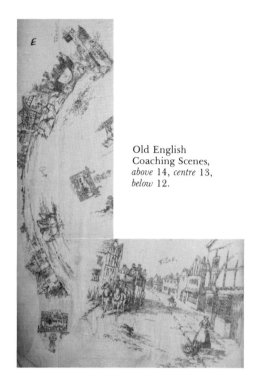

Old English
Coaching Scenes,
above 14, *centre* 13,
below 12.

Old English Coaching Scenes. *Above* 11, *centre* 10,
below 9.

Royal Mail Coach. Rack plate, 1.

Royal Mail Coach
SCENES/TITLES
1 Royal Mail coach galloping, horn sounding
2 Harnessing the horses
3 Driver cracking whip, horses trotting
4 Tightening the harness
5 Waving farewell
6 Loading the coach at the rear
7 Driver and guard together
8 Attendant taking horses to water
9 Weary traveller on milestone
10 Coach galloping

PATTERN NUMBERS
D4490, D4498

COLOURWAYS
Polychrome

SHAPES
Rack plate

DATES
This series was introduced in 1925 and
withdrawn by 1940

Royal Mail Coach, *above* 6, *below* 7.

Royal Mail Coach. *Left to right, top to bottom,* 5, 9, 10, 8, 3, 4, 2.

Life On The Ocean Wave

As islanders the British have always had a close affinity with the sea, no place is more than fifty miles from the coast. However it was also a threat to security and as early as the ninth century King Alfred organised the first navy to guard against invasion. By the sixteenth century the discovery of the Americas and the spice route to the East Indies greatly increased the importance of shipping. The British Navy gradually expanded to protect its ever increasing merchant fleet and the cumbersome Tudor galleons were continually improved upon, evolving into the efficient Men of War and fast, sleek East Indiamen of Nelson's day.

Conditions on board naval ships were appalling and the Navy resorted to pressganging, legally carrying off men and forcing them to enlist. Seamen were known as Jack Tars, after their hats made of tarpaulin, and after they retired as 'old salts' or 'old sea dogs', a name originally given to pirates! Sailors were often away for years at a time and it was the custom, on their return, to give their sweethearts a present. In recent years this could well have been a Royal Doulton jug inscribed with a sea-shanty – one of the songs with a rousing chorus sung by the crew as they hauled in the cables.

Nearer to home, a thriving fishing industry developed on the inshore waters of Britain. The men would row or sail out to sea, casting out and hauling in their lines and nets. Back on shore the womenfolk would be working hard, mending nets, sorting out catches and digging for shell-fish in the sand, as well as helping to carry the fish to market. A variety of cargo boats plied their trade from one small port to another; most of their designs were so distinctive that their locale was instantly recognizable – yawls, ketches, barges and many more.

Even today the British fascination with the sea remains as thousands flock to the beach for their holidays or take to the sea in pleasure yachts and dinghies.

Galleons

SCENES/TITLES
1 Profile view galleon, two sails billowing left
2 Three-quarter view galleon, bow forward, five sails billowing left
3 Three-quarter rear view galleon, four sails billowing right
4 Three-quarter view galleon, four sails billowing left
5 Galleon bow forward, two sails billowing right
6 Three-quarter view galleon, bow forward, two sails billowing right
7 As number 4 but with steps to lower deck
8 Three-quarter view galleon, bow forward, three sails billowing right
9 Three-quarter view galleon, bow forward, four sails billowing right
10 Three-quarter rear view galleon with high poop deck, four sails billowing left
11 Galleon, bow forward, two sails blowing forward
12 Galleon, bow forward, eight sails billowing left
13 Profile view galleon, similar to number 1 but without the sail at the top of the central mast
14 Three-quarter view galleon, bow forward, similar to number 6 but with different deck and flag

PATTERN NUMBERS
D317, D318, D353, D391, D393, D408, D409, D633, D669, D670, D671, D672, D676, D763, D792, D810, D895, D1029, D1130, D1249, D1297, D1302, D1778, D1884

BORDERS
Dolphin, gadroon and laurel, bead, Tudor rose, flying gulls, square chain and shell

COLOURWAYS
Polychrome, blue and white

SHAPES
Dame teapot, Ball teapot, Concord jug, Rack

Galleons. Rack plate, *left to right* 2, 1, 3 and Tudor rose border.

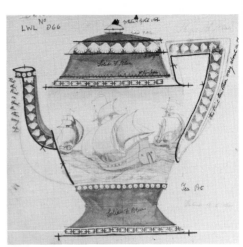

Galleons. *Left to right* 9, 7, 8 and shell, chain and bead borders combined.

Galleons. *Left to right* 5, 4, 6 and dolphin, square chain, seagull and shell borders combined.

Galleons. *Left to right*, 12, 10, 11 and all borders except chain.

Galleons. *Left to right* 14, 13, 3 and square chain and shell border.

plates, round salad bowl, Tavern jug, Breda teapot, Breda jug, Castle jug, Waverley biscuit jar, Melon spittoon, Virginia tobacco jar, Aston biscuit jar, Aston bowl, Durham fern pot, Regent flower bowl, umbrella stand

DATES
This series was introduced in 1886 and extended until 1904. The date of withdrawal is not recorded

Notes Scenes 4 and 5 are found with the quotes: (a) 'Vessels large may venture more. But little boats must hug the shore'; (b) 'The wind that blows the ship that goes and the lass that loves a sailor'

Home Waters
SCENES/TITLES
1 Two sailboats inside stone harbour with row boat in foreground
2 Unloading sailboat *Polly* on far side of wooden pier, two smaller boats nearside and buoy in foreground
3 Unloading two barges at front of stone pier and sheds with chimneys in background
4 Three sailboats rocking in waves at side of wooden pier
5 Several boats sailing past sandy beach
6 Row boat laden with drums being pushed away from stone pier and sailboat being moored by three men. Townscape with domed building in background
7 Three boats unloading at a wooden pier with arched bridge in background
8 Wooden pier with one sailboat in foreground and two smaller ones at side
9 Inside a stone harbour, two row boats in foreground, two sailboats being moored and townscape with domed buildings in background
10 Two sailboats moored by the stern at a stone pier, another sailboat on other side and village in background
11 Two boats sailing, others in background
12 Two sailboats at a wooden pier, one moored by bow, the other by stern. Also smaller sailboat nearby and village scene behind
13 Two boats sailing away from a wooden pier, townscape with domed buildings behind
14 Sailboat moving away from town, another sailboat going in
15 Sailboat pulling down sail, row boat and barge behind
Incidental: Scenes of sailboats for round side of boxes and fruit bowls

Home Waters. Oval plate 5.

Home Waters. 14.

Home Waters. Rack plates, *left to right, top to bottom*, 2, 9, 13, 1, 6, 12, 8, 3, 7.

PATTERN NUMBERS
D6434

COLOURWAYS
Polychrome

SHAPES
Avon teacup and saucer, Rack plates, Avon oval
plate, Avon round dish, tankard, covered box,
cigarette box, cake plate, oval fruit bowl, Avon
fruit, large and small sizes, dish number 8384,
dish number 8382, round fruit bowl with
handles, Arundel earthenware plate, Arundel
teacup and saucer, square plate, tray numbers
7979, 8099, 7923, 7922 and 8237

DATES
This series was introduced in 1954 and
withdrawn in 1967

DESIGNER
W E Grace

SPECIAL BACKSTAMP

Home Waters. 8.

Home Waters. *Left to right* 11, 10.

Home Waters. *Left to right* 15, 4.

Jessopeak Pressgang, 2.

Jessopeak Pressgang. Rack plate, 1.

Jessopeak Pressgang

SCENES/TITLES
1 'The Battle'
2 'The Pressgang'

PATTERN NUMBERS
D2541, D2542, D2761

BORDERS
Stylised leaf

COLOURWAYS
Blue and white, Whieldon ware

SHAPES
Rack plate and unrecorded jug

DATES
This series was introduced in 1906 and
withdrawn by 1930

Notes The Battle scene is often found wrongly
titled as The Pressgang

Old Salt

SCENES/TITLES
1 Three-quarter front view of sailor sculling
row boat
2 Sailor smoking in pub
3 Sailor on creel, lighting pipe

PATTERN NUMBERS
D1979, D3059, D3065

BORDERS
Floats, galleons

COLOURWAYS
Polychrome, blue and white

SHAPES
Rack plates, Tudor jug

DATES
This series was introduced in 1904 and
withdrawn in 1928

DESIGNER
C J Noke and W Nunn

SPECIAL BACKSTAMP

Old Salt. Rack plates, *left to right* 1, 2.

Old Salt, 3.

Old Sea Dogs

SCENES/TITLES
1 'They all love Jack'
2 'Jack's the Boy for Play'
3 'Jack's the Lad for Work'
4 'His Heart is like the Sea'

PATTERN NUMBERS
D2019, D2160

COLOURWAYS
Polychrome, sepia

SHAPES
Unlisted jug

DATES
This series was introduced in 1904. The date of withdrawal is not known but would have been before 1936

DESIGNER
C J Noke

SPECIAL BACKSTAMP

Old Sea Dogs, 4.

Old Sea Dogs. Jugs, *left to right* 2, 3, 1.

Sea Shanty. Jug, 1.

Sea Shanty. Jug, 2.

Sea Shanty

SCENES/TITLES

1 *Three sailors on a pier*
'We were the boys to make her go –
With a hoodah and a doodah
Around the Cape Stiff in frost and snow –
Hooday, hooday, day!

Blow, bo-oys blow, for Californi-o!
There's plenty of gold, so I've been told
On the banks of Sacramento

Verse on the side
'Call all hands to man the capstan
See the cable run down clear

Heave away, and with a will, boys,
For old England we will steer!

Rolling home, rolling home,
Rolling home across the sea,
Rolling home to merrie England,
Rolling home, dear land, to thee!'

2 *Sailor bidding farewell to sweetheart*
'Oh Say, were you ever in Ri-o Grande
O you Rio!
It's there that the river runs down golden sand
And we're bound for the Rio Grande!
O fare you well my bonny young girl –
For we're bound for the Rio Grande!'

PATTERN NUMBERS
D5847, D5887

COLOURWAYS
Polychrome

SHAPES
Rack plate, unrecorded jug, cigarette box

DATES
This series was introduced in 1927. The date of withdrawal is not recorded, but would have been before 1967.

Ships A

SCENES/TITLES
1 Profile view, trading ketch sailing right
2 Profile view, trading ketch sailing left
3 Three-quarter view, trading ketch sailing right
4 Profile view, gaff cutter sailing left
5 Three-quarter view, scaffie sailing right
6 Three-quarter view, trading ketch sailing left towards a trading boat with lateen sail inscribed *DOULTON 1908*
7 Profile view, fishing boat sailing left towards a sloop with sails set
8 Profile view, ketch sailing in choppy seas

PATTERN NUMBERS
D2814, D2872, D2959, D3041, D3063, D3290, D3350, D3643

BORDERS
Grapevine

COLOURWAYS
Polychrome, Holbein

SHAPES
Rack plates, Lennox flower bowl, square and round Leeds fruit dishes, Concord jug, round salad bowl, Burton bowl, Durham fern pot, Virginia tobacco jar, safety matchstand, candlesticks 7227, 7054, Dutch and Pelican, loving cups 7058 and 7116, Breda teaset, Rheims tea cup and saucer, Aldwych and Mayfair toilet sets

DATES
This series was introduced in 1907 and withdrawn by 1932

Ships C, 2

Ships A, 8.

Ships A, *top to bottom, left to right,* 1, 2, 3, 4, 5, 6, 7

Ships B

SCENES/TITLES
1 A group of four trading boats, one laden and with gaff-sail set
2 Three-quarter view of two trading boats, gaff-rigged

PATTERN NUMBERS
D2551, D2559

BORDERS
Plain band

COLOURWAYS
Polychrome

SHAPES
Rack plates

DATES
This series was introduced in 1906 and withdrawn by 1930

Ships C

SCENES/TITLES
1 A yawl, three-quarter view, sailing left
2 Three-quarter view, a trading sloop sailing left

PATTERN NUMBERS
D2273, D2274, D2959

COLOURWAYS
Pink and Blue slip painting

SHAPES
Aubrey toilet set, Mayfair toilet set, Regent bowl, Corinth jug, Pelican trinket set

DATES
This series was introduced in 1908 and withdrawn by 1930

Ships C, 1

Ships B, *left to right* 2, 1

Rural England

For such a small area, the British Isles has a remarkable variety of landscape, from bleak mountains to lush meadows, moorland to forests. While much of this is a result of nature, man and the farmer in particular, has had a singular effect in altering the shape of the land and for centuries life in the country revolved around the farming year.

In ancient and medieval times the real winter began after Christmas, as the fresh meat gave way to dried and salted. While the fields lay frozen the ditches would be cleared, hedgerows cut back and wood gathered. In the early months of the year the ground would be ploughed and sowed. The development of the plough itself made a great difference to farming output; at one time oxen were used but later horses largely took over the task. At the end of the summer the corn crop would be harvested with scythes and after it had been sheaved women and children would glean the remains, that is gather up the ears of corn which had been missed by the reapers.

Life could be hard in the country and there were practical reasons for everything that was done. The lovely thatched cottages made use of nearby reed beds or straw, and the cottage gardens grew vegetables and herbs as well as flowers. Many areas had a local witch, usually a woman skilled in the use of herbal medicine.

While some farmworkers such as milkmaids, ploughmen and shepherds were employed full-time, others were seasonal workers, travelling around the country following the work; fruit-picking in the summer, reaping in the autumn. The gypsies still take such seasonal work and continue to follow their nomadic life.

Sheep were once an important source of England's wealth as the quality of the wool made it sought after all over Europe. Some towns, for instance those close to the Cotswold Hills, owed their prosperity solely to the wool trade. The shepherds were skilled men with only their dogs to help them. On Sundays, and for visits to town, they and the other farmworkers would wear their best smocks of brown holland or hand-made linen. These differed from area to area as each region had its own variant of the honeycomb stitching. A high black hat, called a stove-pipe and a long clay pipe, known as a churchwarden, completed the dress of a 'gaffer', a term of respect for elderly countrymen. In some more isolated parts, regional dress became even more distinctive as with the Welsh and Manx costumes.

Most contact between town and country took place on Market Day. Small, local markets were held at regular intervals, but once a year a larger market might take place, resembling more of a fair. Townsmen often saw their country cousins as being rather slow but the tables could be turned. When some Wiltshire yokels were trying to rescue some smuggled kegs of brandy from a stream they successfully put off the excisemen by pretending to be raking out the cheese (the moon's reflection!) thus creating the legend of the Wiltshire Moonrakers.

Bluebell Gatherers
SCENES/TITLES

1 Woman stooping to pick flowers, basket in left hand
2 Woman and child sitting in bluebells
3 Woman smelling flowers
4 Woman with bundle and child on ground
5 Woman with basket of bluebells in right hand, being loaded by toddler
6 Woman carrying child and basket
7 Woman with basket over her arm
8 Woman bending over to pick flowers, basket in hand
9 Profile view of woman stooping
10 Woman and child sitting in grass
11 Woman stooping
12 Girl in grass with basket

PATTERN NUMBERS
D3567, D3812, E8503

BORDERS
Birds in trees

COLOURWAYS
Polychrome

SHAPES
Rack plates, Joan teaset, unrecorded china vase

DATES
This series was introduced in 1914 and withdrawn by 1928

Bluebell Gatherers.
*Left to right, above 2,
9, 4, 7, 6, below 3,
11, 1, 8, 12, 5.*

Bluebell Gatherers. Rack plates, *left to right, above* 1, 2, 3, *below* 4, 5, 6.

Cotswold Shepherd

CHARACTERS

1 Profile view of shepherd with crook and lantern and dog beside short tree, following sheep towards cottage (cottage not always featured)
2 Rear view of shepherd with dog approaching a group of sheep
3 Rear view of shepherd with dog and sheep outside a cottage with two windows
4 Three-quarter view shepherd standing, his dog sitting at his feet and sheep in distance
5 Shepherd with a lamb in his arm
6 Shepherd sitting under a tree, his dog lying beside him
7 Shepherd sitting under tree, his lantern beside him
8 Profile view of shepherd and dog following a procession of sheep
9 Shepherd sitting under tree talking to lambs
10 Profile view of shepherd carrying twigs
11 Profile view of shepherd with walking stick beside four sheep
12 Profile view of shepherd with lantern and crook, no dog under tree
13 Shepherd sitting on a mound, dog lying in front
14 Shepherd sitting on a mound, lantern on the ground
15 Shepherd followed by dog wagging his tail
16 Profile of shepherd, no dog, following sheep
17 Profile view of shepherd with walking stick followed by dog
18 Profile view of shepherd with dog following sheep beside tall tree
19 Three-quarter view shepherd with seated dog and sheep in front of a church
20 Rear view of shepherd and dog following sheep towards a cottage with one window

PATTERN NUMBERS
D5561

COLOURWAYS
Polychrome

SHAPES
Rack plates, unlisted coffee set, square plates

DATES
This series was introduced in 1933 and withdrawn in 1950

Cotswold Shepherd, 6.

Cotswold Shepherd. *Top to bottom,* 12, 14, 20, 13, 15, 16.

Cotswold Shepherd.
Rack plate and
coffee pot, *left to right* 4, 5.

Cotswold Shepherd.
Plates and teapot,
left to right 1, 3, 2.

Cotswold Shepherd. 9.

Cotswold Shepherd. 7.

Cotswold Shepherd. *Above* 10, *below* 11.

Cotswold Shepherd. *From top to bottom* 18, 17, 3, 19.

Country Garden. *Left to right, above* 5, 3, *below,* 4, 2, 6, 7.

Country Garden, 6.

Country Garden
SCENES/TITLES
1 Milkmaid with yoke
2 Milkmaid with stool and bucket
3 Maid at well
4 Maid at water pump
5 Old lady with basket and stick
6 Old man with scythe
7 Girl feeding chickens

PATTERN NUMBERS
D4932, D5429, D5825

COLOURWAYS
Polychrome

SHAPES
Rack plate, square teaplate, stein, unrecorded jug

DATES
This series was introduced in 1929. The date of withdrawal is not recorded

Country Garden, Rack plate and ash-tray, *left to right* 2, 1.

Country Sayings. Rack plates, *left to right* 2, 1, 3.

Country Sayings

SCENES/TITLES
1 'Now I have a sheep and a cow everybody
  bids me good-morrow'
2 'They who won't be counselled can't be
  helped'
3 'If you bring a smiling visage to the glass you
  meet a smile'

PATTERN NUMBERS
D5103

BORDERS
Scroll, fleur de lys leaves

COLOURWAYS
Polychrome

SHAPES
Rack plate, Tudor jug, unrecorded stein

DATES
This series was introduced in 1931. The date of
withdrawal is not recorded but it was probably
discontinued during World War II

Countryside. 3.

Countryside. *Left to right* 2, 1.

Countryside. Rack plates, *left to right, from top to bottom* 5, 13, 6, 8, 11, 10, 4, 12, 7, 9.

Countryside
SCENES/TITLES
1 Cottage, woman in doorway, another
   drawing water
2 The grocer's cottage
3 Cottage with children playing on road
   outside
4 Cottage, with dormer windows and porch,
   two people on path
5 Cottage behind bridge, church beside
6 Group of cottages, old man and old woman
   chatting
7 The watermill
8 Cottage with garden plot in front
9 Cottage with two hayricks
10 Cottage on a hill
11 Cottage with bridge on stilts
12 Cottage with porch, fence around
13 A village

PATTERN NUMBERS
D3647, D5688

COLOURWAYS
Polychrome

SHAPES
Joan teaset, Concord jug, Regent flower bowl,
tobacco jar, Sherwood flower bowl, Octagon
fruit dish, teapot stand, Leeds round fruit dish,
Mayfair toilet set, round salad bowl

DATES
This series was introduced in 1912, extended in
1936 and withdrawn by 1945

Elderly Farmworkers. Character 1.

Elderly Farmworkers
SCENES/TITLES
1 'He hath most who coveteth least'

CHARACTERS
1 Old man with scythe
2 Old man with rake

PATTERN NUMBERS
D3511, D3515

COLOURWAYS
Polychrome

SHAPES
Don jug

DATES
This series was introduced in 1911. The date of
withdrawal is not recorded but would have been
by 1936

Elderly Farmworkers. Character 2.

English Cottages.
Rack plates, *left to
right* A2, A1.

English Cottages. *Above* A5, *below* A3.

English Cottages. A4.

English Cottages A

SCENES/TITLES
1 A group of cottages behind a stream with
  wooden bridge
2 Thatched cottage with timbered gable-end
  behind stream
3 Large thatched cottage with two wings
4 House with elaborate timbered gable-end
5 L-shaped thatched cottage
6 Cottage by a path

PATTERN NUMBERS
D4390, D4987, H3423, H3915, H3916

COLOURWAYS
Polychrome

SHAPES
Rack plate, Breda teaset, Quorn teaset

DATES
This series was introduced in 1924, extended in
1929 and 1941. The date of withdrawal is not
recorded

English Cottages. A6.

English Cottages. *Left to right* B1, B2.

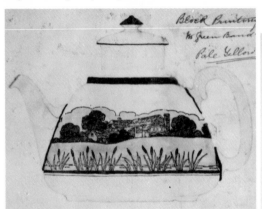

English Cottages. B3.

English Cottages B

SCENES/TITLES
1 Two cottages with bullrushes in foreground
2 Cottage with lean-to and bullrushes in foreground
3 Large cottage with prominent chimney stack

PATTERN NUMBERS
D3306, D3307, D3478

COLOURWAYS
Polychrome, celadon

SHAPES
Joan teaset

DATES
This series was introduced in 1910. The date of withdrawal is not recorded but it would have been before 1936

Farming. Silhouette. Rack plate, 1.

Farming Silhouette

SCENES/TITLES
1 Shepherd with crook holding lamb, sheep at feet
2 Two adults and three children laden with bundles
3 Man driving plough
4 Woman with sheep
5 Woman loading wheelbarrow
6 Shepherd with crook and lantern
7 Man in haycart
8 Man on horseback leading another horse
9 Man sawing

Farming. Silhouette. *From top to bottom* 2, 3, 4, 5.

Farming. Silhouette. *Left to right, above* 9, 7, *below* 8, 6.

PATTERN NUMBERS
D3577, D3598, D3601

COLOURWAYS
Polychrome, Holbein

SHAPES
Rack plate, Joan teaset and stand, Leeds round fruit bowl, round salad bowl, tobacco jar, York sandwich trays, Pelican, Dutch and 7227 candlesticks, spittoon, loving cup 7058, jug 7198, Lennox flower bowl, stein, matchstriker

DATES
This series was introduced in 1912. The date of withdrawal is not recorded but it would have been before 1936

Farmworkers – Silhouette
SCENES/TITLES
1 Shepherd wearing wide brimmed hat with crook
2 Shepherd with crook
3 Reaper

PATTERN NUMBERS
D3356

COLOURWAYS
Polychrome, Holbein

SHAPES
Rack plates, tobacco jar, Corinth teaset, vase numbers 7317 and 7318

DATES
This series was introduced in 1910 and withdrawn by 1930

Farmworkers. Silhouette. Rack plates, *left to right* 1, 3, 2.

Fireside. Characters *left to right, above* 4, 6, *centre* 3, 7, *below* 2.

Fireside

SCENES/TITLES
1 Fireside scene with door to right and cat
2 Fireside scene with tea table to the left
3 Fireside scene with settle under window

CHARACTERS
1 Old lady with baby
2 Old lady with cat
3 Old lady sewing sock
4 Old lady mending, facing left
5 Old lady mending, facing right
6 Old man reading with dog facing right
7 Old man reading with dog facing left

PATTERN NUMBERS
D4570

BORDERS
Brown band

COLOURWAYS
Polychrome

SHAPES
Rack plates, Windmill teaset, Astor celery tray, New Empire teaset

DATES
This series was introduced in 1925 and withdrawn by 1942

DESIGNER
C J Noke

Fireside. Rack plates, *left to right* Character 5 with scene 2, Character 1 with scene 1.

Gaffers. Rack plates, *left to right, above* 8, 2, 16, *below* 5, 3, 7.

Gaffers. Jugs and teaset, *left to right* 9, 1, 15, 11, 12, 16.

Gaffers. *Left to right, above* 14, 9, 13, 17, *centre* 11, *below* 5, 4, 6 10, 7.

Gaffers. 18.

Gaffers 19.

Gaffers

CHARACTERS

1 Front view of gaffer with two hands leaning on stick
2 Front view of gaffer with left hand holding angled stick
3 Front view of gaffer with bundle in left hand, stick in the other
4 Front view of gaffer with umbrella under left arm, stick in other hand
5 Front view of gaffer with one hand stroking his chin, the other holding up cane
6 Front view of gaffer in buttoned smock with left hand holding angled stick
7 Profile view of gaffer facing left with both hands on stick
8 Profile view of gaffer facing right with one hand on stick, other holding basket
9 Profile view of gaffer smoking
10 Three-quarter view of gaffer with one hand in his pocket, the other holding angled stick
11 Three-quarter view of gaffer with right hand holding basket, the other leaning on vertical stick
12 Three-quarter view of gaffer with right hand holding basket, the other leaning on angled stick
13 Three-quarter view of gaffer with umbrella under right arm and two hands clasped round it
14 Three-quarter view of gaffer with bundle under right arm, resting on umbrella in left hand
15 Three-quarter view of gaffer wearing buttoned smock with bundle under right arm and walking with umbrella in left hand
16 Three-quarter view of gaffer with bundle under left arm and umbrella in right hand
17 Two old men talking
18 Gaffer and his wife
19 Front view of gaffer with bundle in right hand, holding stick in front with left hand

PATTERN NUMBERS
D4210

COLOURWAYS
Polychrome

SHAPES
Rack plates, York sandwich tray, beaker, Pelican powder box and puff box, Pelican candlestick, Cleveland teaset, Corinth jug, Rheims tea cup and saucer, New Empire teaset, Cecil jam, Argus jug, Cheshire cheese dish, round fruit saucer, oatmeal saucer, porridge plate, Melbourne sandwich tray, Leeds round fruit dish, Octagon sweet dish, round salad bowl, New rim, Napier, Ancester and 89 ashtrays, Lennox flower bowl, Westcott jug, Newlyn jug, teapot stand, Virginia tobacco jar, vase numbers 7397, 7385, 7432, 7347, 7538b, 7444, 7532, 7348, 7493, 7331, 7386

DATES
This series was introduced in 1921 and withdrawn by 1949

DESIGNER
C J Noke

SPECIAL BACKSTAMP

Notes Some characters are accompanied by the inscription: 'I be all the way from Zummerset where the zyder apples grows'

Gleaners and Gypsies. Rack plates, *left to right, above* 16, 11, 17, *below* 18, 10, 12.

Gleaners and Gypsies. Teaset, *left to right* 7, 3, 14.

Gleaners and Gypsies. Jug and plate, *left to right* 5, 6.

Gleaners and Gypsies. Rack plates, *left to right* 1, 2, with birds in tree-tops border.

Gleaners and Gypsies

SCENES/TITLES

1 Campfire scene
2 Man leading donkey with his family
3 Woman and boy pulling sledge, dog in background
4 Woman and girl dragging bale of hay
5 Woman sitting on a rock
6 Standing woman pointing to stooping woman
7 Woman with bundle of corn at hip. Girl with corn on back and boy
8 Woman standing with corn and hand on hip, another stooping
9 Woman and child sitting on grass, man gathering corn
10 Woman with child clinging to skirts and boy balancing corn on shoulder
11 Woman tying a bundle of corn to boy's back
12 One woman stooping, another kneeling
13 Woman with boy holding her bundle and girl with corn on head
14 One woman standing with bundle, another stooping
15 Man and woman kneeling in fields gathering
16 Boy climbing fence, woman with bundle behind
17 Rear view woman with bundle on head and boy with bundle in arms
18 Front view woman with bundle on head, more corn in apron, and girl
19 Woman standing with bundle, man gathering behind
20 Woman sitting, woman with bundle on back behind
21 Woman sitting with corn in lap, man with bundle in arms, rear view
22 Rear view woman holding boy's hand, girl with bundle on head
23 Woman with bundle in arms, girl with bundle on head

PATTERN NUMBERS
D3191, D3554, D3812, D3821, D4842, D4853, D4854, D4983, D4984, D5003, D5356, D5624, D5810, D6123

BORDERS
Tulip and scroll, scroll, birds in tree tops, basket weave

COLOURWAYS
Polychrome

SHAPES
Rack plates, Durham fern bowl, York sandwich tray, Vase number 7493, Regent fern bowl, Ball teaset, Loving cup number 7038, Dutch candlestick, tobacco jar, spittoon, round salad bowl, Royles teapot, Westcott jug, Mayfair jug, Pelican candlesticks, Louis dessert plate, chop dish, stein

DATES
This series was introduced in 1909, the range was extended until 1937 and withdrawn by 1955

DESIGNER
S Wilson

SPECIAL BACKSTAMP

Notes Scene 5 is found on a special plate to commemorate the Coronation of 1911

Gleaners and Gypsies. *Left to right, top to bottom* 19, 20, 22, 21, 23, 8.

Gleaners and Gypsies. *Top to bottom* 9, 4, 15, 13.

Haystacks. 1.

Haystacks

SCENES/TITLES
Haystacks with a church in the background

PATTERN NUMBERS
D2538

BORDERS
Stylised trees

COLOURWAYS
Holbein

SHAPES
Rack plate

DATES
This series was introduced in 1906. The date of withdrawal is not recorded although it would have been before 1936.

Illustrated Proverbs. *Left to right, above* 1, 2, *below* 3.

Isle of Man. Rack plates and vase, *left to right* 1, 4, 2, 1, 3, 5.

Isle of Man. Vases and box, *left to right* 7, 6, reverse of 6, 5.

Illustrated Proverbs

SCENES/TITLES
1 'Quarrelling dogs come halting home'
2 'A bird in the hand is worth two in the bush'
3 'Fast bind fast find'

CHARACTERS
1 Man using broom as crutch
2 Man with dead goose
3 Man tied to signpost

PATTERN NUMBERS
D1748, D1749, D1750

COLOURWAYS
Polychrome, Holbein

SHAPES
Tavern jug

DATES
This series was introduced in 1903. The date of withdrawal is not recorded but would have been before 1936

Isle of Man. 8.

Isle Of Man

SCENES/TITLES
1 Shepherd with crook and lantern
2 Maid holding apron
3 Old man leaning on a stick
4 Postman delivering a letter to a woman
5 Two old women leaning on sticks
6 Woman carrying two baskets
7 Old man bent over, leaning on a stick
8 Fisherman talking to a woman with basket

PATTERN NUMBERS
Not recorded

COLOURWAYS
Polychrome

SHAPES
Octagon rack plate, oval covered box, vases
numbers 6886 and 9229

DATES
This series was introduced around 1909. The
date of withdrawal is not recorded

SPECIAL BACKSTAMP

Market Day A
SCENES/TITLES
1 Farmer with the landlord at the inn
2 Farmer and his wife in their Sunday best

PATTERN NUMBERS
D3716, D3738

BORDERS
Stylised leaves

COLOURWAYS
Polychrome

SHAPES
Rack plates, Arno jug

DATES
This series was introduced in 1914. The date of
withdrawal is not recorded but it would have
been before 1936

Market Day B
SCENES/TITLES
1 Punch and Judy
2 Market Day
3 Shopping at the market

SHAPES
No shapes have so far been recorded

DATES
This series features in the pattern books of 1954

DESIGNER
W E Grace

Market Day B. 3.

Market Day A. Rack
plates, 1, 2.

Market Day B. *Above* 1, *below* 2.

Open Door. Rack plates, *left to right* 2, 1.

Open Door
SCENES/TITLES
1 Fireplace and open door with cat on right
2 Fireplace, window and open door with cat on left

PATTERN NUMBERS
D3750, D3754, D4538

BORDERS
Dark green band

COLOURWAYS
Polychrome, sepia

SHAPES
Rack plates, Newlyn jug, Leeds oval dish, round salad bowl, square dish, round dish, Clive teapot stand, York sandwich tray, Ancester and Napier ashtrays, Windmill teaset, Quorn teaset

DATES
This series was introduced in 1914 and withdrawn by 1936

Plough Horses – Silhouette

SCENES/TITLES
1 Two horses, one profile, one three-quarter view front in harness
2 Profile horses drinking and two farm workers
3 Group of four horses grazing, farm workers in front
4 Horse following farm hand
5 Two profile horses trotting, overlapping
6 Two horses, profile, one grazing
7 Horse stamping with rear hoof
8 Horse being harnessed
9 Horse and rider
10 Walking horse
11 Group of three horses, two grazing
12 One horse grazing
13 Two horses overlapping, one grazing
14 Two horses in full harness

PATTERN NUMBERS
D2552, D2777, D2813, D2825, D2878, D2937

BORDERS
Rose, anthemion, trees

COLOURWAYS
Holbein

SHAPES
Rack plate, Mayfair toilet set, round salad bowl, Virginia tobacco jar, spittoon, safety match stand, Lennox flower bowl, jug 7119, unrecorded teapot and stand, Aldwych toilet set

DATES
This series was introduced in 1906 and withdrawn by 1929

Notes 'We'll tak a cup a' kindness yet for days of auld lang syne' inscribed on some examples

Plough horses. Flower bowl, 13.

Plough horses. Flower bowl, 14.

Plough horses. Rack plates, *left to right* 6, 1.

Plough horses. Flower bowl, 12.

Plough horses. *Above* 3, *below* 2.

Plough horses. *Left to right, above* 7, 5 *below* 4, 13.

Plough horses. 8.

Ploughing. *above* 6, *below* 5.

Plough horses. 9, 10.

Ploughing. 4.

Ploughing
SCENES/TITLES
1 Pair of horses pulling plough with farmer steering
2 Ploughman going home with three horses
3 Ploughman adjusting his plough
4 Pair of horses pulling plough, one with head drooping
5 Ploughman with three horses in harness, another pair in the background
6 Side view of ploughman with his pair of horses

PATTERN NUMBERS
D3827, D3854, D4934, D5650

COLOURWAYS
Polychrome

SHAPES
Lennox flower bowl, Mayfair jug, wavy plate

DATES
This series was introduced in 1915 and in 1929. It was withdrawn by 1948

Plough horses. 11.

Ploughing. Rack plates, *left to right* 1, 2, 3.

Romany. Rack plates, *left to right* 2, 3, 1.

Romany. 4.

Romany

SCENES/TITLES
1 Two male and two female gypsies drinking at a wooden table, beside a campfire
2 Woman leading a child on a donkey, caravans in background
3 Campfire with two adults and two children
4 Three adults by a campfire, one holding a baby, a little girl in the foreground, caravans in the background

PATTERN NUMBERS
D5027, D5809

COLOURWAYS
Polychrome

SHAPES
Rack plate, stein, York sandwich tray, shaped tea plate

DATES
This series was introduced in 1930 and withdrawn in 1945

98

Rural Churches.
Rack plates, *left to right* 2, 1.

Rural Churches
SCENES/TITLES
1 Square towered church beside cottages, lambs in the foreground
2 Church with steeple and cottages in the trees, lambs in the foreground

PATTERN NUMBERS
D2846

COLOURWAYS
Holbein

SHAPES
Rack plate, Tudor jug, Windmill teaset, Lennox flower bowl

DATES
This series was introduced in 1907. The date of withdrawal is not recorded but it would have been before 1936

Notes Occasionally the lambs do not appear

Rustic England
SCENES/TITLES
1 Horse being shod
2 Hounds leaping fence in front of cottage
3 Cart at the toll house
4 Farmer waving stick at cows and sheep
5 Three girls on a stile holding twigs
6 Man with bundle on stick on the route to London
7 Haycart with chickens in foreground
8 Mending rush chair
9 Harvesting
10 Boy pulling bundle of sticks
11 Shepherd and sheep
12 Thatched barn

PATTERN NUMBERS
D5694, D5942, D6297

COLOURWAYS
Polychrome

Rustic England.
Rack plates, *left to right* 8, 3.

Rustic England. Plates and box, *left to right* 1, 5, 2.

Rustic England. *Left to right, above* 11, 7, *below* 12, 4.

SHAPES
Rack plates, Octagon fruit dish, Leeds oval fruit dish, fruit saucer, coupe, square tea plate, Dorothy plate, Devon comport, Arundel plate, Winchester salad bowl, trays 8051 and 8237 vase numbers 7958, 8186a, 8187, 8188, 8224, 8330, 8150, 8331, 8190, 8160, 8246

DATES
This series was introduced in 1936 and extended in 1949. It was withdrawn in 1960.

DESIGNER
W E Grace

Rustic England. *Above* 9, *centre* 6, *below* 5, 10.

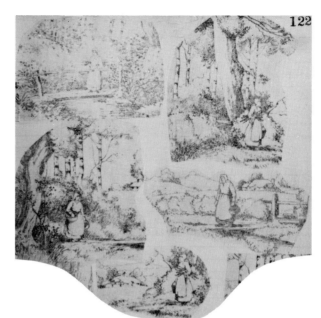

Springtime. *Left to right, above* 1, 2, *below* 4, 5, 3.

Springtime. Rack plates, *from top to bottom* 5, 2, 4, 6.

Springtime

SCENES/TITLES
1 Old lady with twigs crossing bridge
2 Old lady with twigs under right arm and bucket
3 Old lady with twigs under left arm, cottage behind
4 Old lady with basket in each hand walking out of wood
5 Old lady with basket walking along road in front of cottage
6 Old woman with child on bridge

PATTERN NUMBERS
D4933

COLOURWAYS
Polychrome

SHAPES
Rack plates, round salad bowl

DATES
This series was introduced in 1929. The date of withdrawal is not recorded.

Summertime in England. *Left to right, above* 4, 1, 2, 5, *below* 2, 5, 3, 5.

Summertime in England, 6.

Summertime In England
SCENES/TITLES
1 Stream and cottages in foreground, castle on hill
2 Wooden railed bridge across a stream, cottages behind
3 Arched stone bridge with cottages behind
4 Cottages in foreground, stone bridge in background
5 Part of wooden fence with cottages behind
6 Cottages and church

PATTERN NUMBERS
D6131

COLOURWAYS
Polychrome

SHAPES
Rack plate, Dame teaset, shaped plates

DATES
This series was introduced in 1941. The date of withdrawal is not recorded but it would have been before 1967

Welsh. Rack plates, *left to right* 9, 1, 16.

Welsh. Jug, 15.

Welsh. Rack plate, 17.

Welsh. *Left to right, from top to bottom* 8, 2, 10, 3, 15, 5, 4, 7, 11, 6, 14, 13.

Welsh. 12.

Welsh

CHARACTERS
1 Woman with umbrella and hand in pocket
2 Two women in cloaks chatting
3 Woman giving a flower to another
4 Two women and a dog
5 Old woman holding child's hand
6 Child running to woman with cane
7 Woman with basket chatting to woman with arms folded
8 Three seated women listening to the tale of another
9 Three women and child walking to chapel, woman and child in distance
10 Woman with basket leaning on fence
11 Girl running to seated woman
12 Three women walking, further along two single women with baskets
13 Woman with arms outstretched talking to another
14 Two women approaching another with hands raised
15 Woman with hand on hip, another nearby
16 Woman with basket over left arm
17 Bust of Welsh woman

PATTERN NUMBERS
D2717, D3363, D5914, E3794, E3806

BORDERS
Lacy flower

COLOURWAYS
Polychrome

SHAPES
Rack plates, miniature vases, fluted oval dish, vase 7493, Lennox flower bowl, Westcott jug, jugs 6061 and 7040, Windmill teapot

DATES
This series was introduced in 1906 and extended in 1911 and 1938. The date of withdrawal is not recorded but it was probably during World War II

DESIGNER
C J Noke

Wiltshire Moonrakers. Rack plate, 1.

Wiltshire Moonrakers. *From top to bottom* 2, 3, 4, 5, *on the right* 6.

Wiltshire Moonrakers

SCENES/TITLES
1 Two men raking in pond and explaining to customs official
'We'm raking out that cheese, zur'
2 Two men talking, one with rake under his arm
3 Three men talking beside rakes and barrels
4 Two men by the pond
5 Three men at pub door
6 Procession of moonrakers and smuggled booty

PATTERN NUMBERS
D4625

COLOURWAYS
Polychrome

SHAPES
Rack plates, Westcott jug, Cleveland teaset

DATES
This series was introduced in 1926 and withdrawn by 1946

SPECIAL BACKSTAMP
'Down "Vizes way" in days of old
The "Sizemen" then were proper sold
To zee a crazy headed loon
Rake at the shadder of the moon'

Witches

SCENES/TITLES
1 Witch crouched by cauldron adding ingredients
2 Witch standing to the left of cauldron adding ingredients

PATTERN NUMBERS
D2505, D2673, D2735, D2903, D3400

BORDERS
Leaf, tendril and dot, scallop shell and scroll, laurel and Greek key

COLOURWAYS
Sepia and green, Holbein

SHAPES
Rack plate, safety match stand, Low teaset, Nimrod teapot

DATES
This series was introduced in 1906 and withdrawn by 1928

Witches. Rack plate, 2.

Witches. 1.

Woodland

SCENES/TITLES
1 Two cottages and church in rolling landscape
2 Two cottages in landscape
3 One cottage in landscape

PATTERN NUMBERS
D3040, D3186, D4585, D5815, E7178

COLOURWAYS
Polychrome, Whieldon

SHAPES
Rack plate, unrecorded bowl, Mayfair toilet set, round salad bowl, Virginia tobacco jar, Breda jug

DATES
This series was introduced in 1908, redrawn in 1937 and withdrawn in 1956

Woodland. Rack plates, *left to right* 1, 1, 3, 2.

Zunday Zmocks. *Top to bottom* 3, 4, 5.

Zunday Zmocks. Rack plate, 1.

Zunday Zmocks
CHARACTERS
1 Front view of man on left, profile of man on right
2 Front view of two old men smiling, ivy creeping up wall
3 Single smiling man under a large blossom tree
4 Front view of smiling man under a small tree
5 Front view of two old men smiling
6 Front view of man on left with neckerchief, profile view of man on right

7 Three-quarter view of man on left, profile of man on right
8 Profile of man on left, three-quarter view of man on right in patterned smock
9 Profile of man on left, three-quarter view of man on right
10 Three-quarter view of man on left, profile of man on right behind short wall

PATTERN NUMBERS
D5680

SHAPES
Quorn teaset

DATES
This series was introduced in 1936 and withdrawn by 1950

DESIGNER
C J Noke

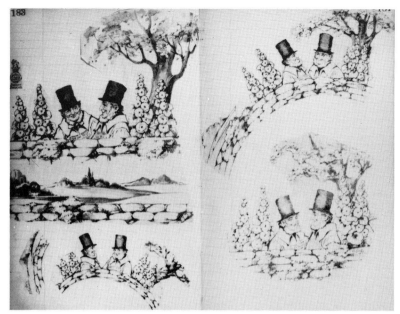

Zunday Zmocks. *Left to right, above* 6, 9, *below* 8, 7.

Zunday Zmocks. *Left to right* 2, 10.

Sport and Leisure

In medieval times falconry was a favourite sport of the rich, together with the hunting of stags and hares. Fox hunting, that most English of sports, did not become established until the late seventeenth century. The hunt begins with a meet where a stirrup-cup may be offered and is led by the Master, Huntsmen and Whippers-In, who control the hounds and take precedence over the field. The uniform, of coloured coat and individual hunt buttons, can only be worn by invitation and it is considered a great honour to be granted that privilege. The famous John Peel (1776–1854) was Master of his own pack in the north of England but the best-known hunts are further south, such as the Quorn in Leicestershire.

On the open Scottish moors large shoots are held, where partridge and grouse are retrieved by trained gun-dogs. Deerstalking is another popular Highland sport which demands great skill and today many take pleasure in showing their prowess by 'shooting' the stag with a camera rather than a gun.

It was the Scots who invented golf, one of the most popular sports of today. In 1457 King James II of Scotland decreed that both "Fute-ball and Golfe be utterly cryed downe" because they interfered with archery-practice but obviously his words were in vain as some of the best golf-courses in the world are still to be found north of the border. For those who enjoy the quiet life, fishing is as popular today as it ever was.

Winter is traditionally the season for ice-skating, although with the modern rinks it is no longer necessary to wait for ponds to freeze. In the summer, millions head for the sea and sun, but sunbathing is a relatively modern pastime popularised in the 1920's. The seaside merry-go-rounds enjoyed by children today developed from the travelling fairs which once provided great entertainment for country folks, with side-shows and games which are virtually lost today. Although we still dance around the May-pole, who amongst us has ever chased a pig or climbed a slippery pole?

Falconry. Rack plate, 9.

Falconry

CHARACTERS

1. Two horsemen and man standing with bugles and dogs
2. Two men and one lady on horseback passing a peasant with sheep
3. Horseman pointing ahead, lady riding at side
4. Lady galloping, patterned skirts this side, man on other side
5. Man blowing horn, lady galloping at side
6. Lady galloping, man with horn swinging from shoulders
7. Gentleman galloping looking back at lady
8. Lady galloping looking back at man
9. Three ladies galloping with man and falcon
10. Lady and gentleman galloping with man and falcon
11. Lady with gentleman holding falcon, another man on inside
12. Lady trotting, skirts this side, profile view
13. Gentleman trotting, profile view
14. Lady galloping, skirts far side, scarf trailing, three-quarter view
15. Lady galloping, skirts this side, scarf trailing, profile view

16 Lady galloping, three-quarter view, skirts this side
17 Lady galloping, three-quarter view, skirts this side, holding a crop
18 Lady galloping, skirts this side, profile view
19 Gentleman galloping, cloak flying, profile view
20 Gentleman galloping waving horn
21 Gentleman galloping waving whip
22 Gentleman galloping, profile view
23 Lady galloping, skirts this side, man on other side, both in plumed hats
24 Gentleman and lady in tall pointed hat and veil
25 Lady galloping, profile view, wearing large black plumed hat

PATTERN NUMBERS
D3696, D3916

BORDERS
Castle, scroll and diaper

COLOURWAYS
Polychrome

SHAPES
Rack plate, Newlyn jug, round salad bowl

DATES
This series was introduced in 1913 and withdrawn by 1930

SPECIAL BACKSTAMP

Falconry. *Left to right, top to bottom* 24, 1, 9, 2, 4.

Falconry. *Left to right, top to bottom* 8, 6, 12, 25, 7, 13, 5, 11.

Fox Hunting A

SCENES/TITLES
1 The hunt meeting a donkey and cart
2 Dismounted huntsman under the hedge
3 Huntsman in a duck pond
4 The hunt startling a ploughman and his horses
5 The hunt chasing the fox
6 Huntsman caught in a tree

PATTERN NUMBERS
D5104, D5879, D5882, D5948

COLOURWAYS
Polychrome

SHAPES
Rack plates, vases numbers: 7745, 8149, 8150, 8151

DATES
The series was introduced in 1931 and the range was added to until 1938. It was withdrawn by 1950

Falconry. *Left to right, top to bottom* 22, 16, 15, 23, 18, 19, 14, 21, 17, 20, 3, 10.

Fox hunting. A3.

Fox hunting. A4.

Fox hunting. Jug, B2, B4.

Fox hunting. Lid, B1, ash-trays, *left to right* B3, B4, B2, B4.

Fox hunting. Rack plates, *from top to bottom* A5, A6, A2, A1.

Fox hunting. C3.

Fox Hunting B
SCENES/TITLES
1 Mounted huntsman leaping ditch
2 Running fox
3 Walking fox
4 Running hounds

PATTERN NUMBERS
D5595, D5656, D5909

SHAPES
Relief jug, cigarette box and trays, square
teaplate

DATES
This series was introduced in 1935. The date of
withdrawal is not recorded

Fox Hunting C
SCENES/TITLES
1 'The fox is shot, sir'
2 'The game old fox'
3 'Here's to that fox'

PATTERN NUMBERS
D2290

COLOURWAYS
Polychrome

SHAPES
Tavern Jug

DATES
This series was introduced in 1905 and would
have been withdrawn by 1928

DESIGNER
W Nunn

Fox hunting. *Above* C1, *below* C2.

COLOURWAYS
Polychrome

SHAPES
Special relief shaped teaset, jugs and tankards

DATES
This series was introduced in 1930 and
withdrawn by 1946

Fox hunting – relief
SCENES/TITLES
1 Fox hiding behind tree
2 Fox with scarecrow
3 Fox and hounds
4 Hounds and cockerell
5 Huntsmen and hounds
6 Fox hiding up a tree
7 Huntsman with the brush
8 Huntsman jumping fence

PATTERN NUMBERS
D4988, D5595

Fox hunting – relief, 6.

Fox hunting – relief. Coffee set, *left to right* 2, 5, 4, 3, 1.

Fox hunting – relief. Tankard and jug, *left to right* 8, 7.

Fox Mottoes

SCENES/TITLES
1 'A fox should not be on the jury at a goose's trial'
2 'An old fox needs not to be taught tricks'
3 'Foxes never fare better than when they are cursed'

PATTERN NUMBERS
D3567

BORDERS
Oak leaf

COLOURWAYS
Polychrome

SHAPES
Arno jug

DATES
This series was introduced in 1912 and withdrawn by 1928

Fox mottoes. *Left* 3, *right, above* 2, *below* 1.

Hunting. *Above* A2, *below* A3.

Hunting A

SCENES/TITLES
1 Two huntsmen, one whipping in hounds
2 Profile view of two huntsmen, leader waving whip
3 Huntslady and huntsman with hounds

PATTERN NUMBERS
D1483, D1484

BORDERS
Stylised trees

COLOURWAYS
Polychrome

SHAPES
Unrecorded jug similar to Breda

DATES
This series was introduced in 1903 and withdrawn by 1928

Hunting. A1.

Hunting. Rack plate, B3.

Hunting. B2.

Hunting B

SCENES/TITLES
1 Fireside scene
2 Dismounted huntsman with hounds, mounted huntsman brandishing his hat
3 Dismounted huntsman by tree
4 Huntsman leaping fallen gate
5 Huntsman mounted walking with dogs
6 Lady on horseback leaping fence

PATTERN NUMBERS
D4800, D4805, D5056, D5057, D5868, D5908

BORDERS
Flute and scroll, Basket weave

COLOURWAYS
Polychrome

SHAPES
Octagonal rack plates, shaped plates

DATES
This series was introduced in 1928 and the range was added to until 1938. The date of withdrawal is not known but it was probably during World War II

Hunting C

SCENES/TITLES
1 Two huntsmen leaping hedge
2 Two mounted huntsmen with hounds
3 Whipper-in with hounds
4 Galloping huntsman with hounds

PATTERN NUMBERS
D4995, D5075

BORDERS
Embossed trees and fruit

COLOURWAYS
Polychrome

SHAPES
Shaped plates

DATES
This series was introduced in 1930 and withdrawn by 1946

Hunting. *Left to right, above,* B5 B4, *below* B6, B1.

Hunting. C2.

Hunting. C1.

Hunting. Rack plate, C3.

Hunting. C4.

Hunting – John Peel

SCENES/TITLES
1 Two huntsmen leading two horses
2 Two mounted huntsmen raising hats
3 Lady and little boy on horseback
4 Innkeeper carrying tray of beer from inn
5 Wench serving two huntsmen
6 Woman serving three huntsmen
7 Lady on horseback with gentlemen beside
8 Huntsman galloping with hounds
9 Huntsman coming through a gate

PATTERN NUMBERS
D4340, D4892, D4893, D6231, H2620,
H2866

COLOURWAYS
Polychrome

SHAPES
Rack plate, Quorn teaset, shaped teaplates,
unrecorded bone china shapes

DATES
This series was introduced in 1924 and added
to in 1947. The date of withdrawal is not
recorded.

Hunting. John Peel. Rack plates, *top
to bottom* 8, 2 & 3, 5 & 4, 1.

Hunting. John Peel. 9.

Hunting. John Peel. *Above* 6, *below* 7.

Hunting – Morland

SCENES/TITLES

1 Huntsman galloping and waving his whip over his head
2 Lone huntsman looking for the hunt
3 Huntsman galloping and pointing ahead with his whip
4 Huntslady galloping, her skirts falling this side of the horse
5 Whipper-in urging on the hounds
6 Galloping huntsman holding his whip aloft
7 Galloping huntsman waving his crop
8 Huntslady galloping, her skirts on the far side of her horse
9 Two huntsmen, one with his head hidden in the trees
10 Huntsman pointing with his hat
11 Three galloping horsemen
12 Group of three horses, one without a rider
13 Huntsman, looking down from his horse

PATTERN NUMBERS
D800, D801, D941, D1031, D1040, D1072, D1074, D1080, D1081, D1129, D1228, D1229, D1234, D1267, D1273, D1314, D1315, D1320, D1321, D1323, D1324, D1375, D1376, D1391, D1392, D1448, D1449, D1553, D1557, D1659, D1664, D1665, D1698, D1699, D1700, D1701, D1702, D1729, D1730, D1733, D1779, D1845, D2040, D2099, D3042, D3106, D3636

BORDERS
Vine, foliate, oriel, stylised leaf, flower and lace, gilt flower, ivy, shell, flower and spade, gadroon and laurel, fruit and swag, stylised flower, scroll and bird

COLOURWAYS
Polychrome, blue and white, Holbein, Whieldon, maroon and yellow

SHAPES
Rack plates, Ball teaset, Romola teaset, Low teaset, Tavern jug, Tudor jug, Castle jug, Dundee jug, Arden jug, Breda jug, Aubrey toilet set, Flagon toilet set, Virginia tobacco jar, Paris biscuit jar, Leeds biscuit jar, Cantor biscuit jar, unrecorded cachepot

DATES
This series was introduced in 1901 and the range was added to until 1913. It was withdrawn by 1928

DESIGNER
After designs by George Morland (1763–1804)

SPECIAL BACKSTAMP

Notes Occasionally mottoes are found on this series. For example: (a) 'Why hesitate – too soon is better than too late'; (b) 'Among good fellows every toast will pass that serves to carry round another glass'; (c) 'The more the merrier, the fewer the better cheer'

Hunting – Morland. *Above* 11, *centre* 13, *below* 12.

Hunting – Morland. Rack plates, *left to right, above* 2, 6, 4, *below* 5, 3, 7.

Hunting – Morland. *Above* 9, *below* 10.

Hunting – Morland. Jug, 1.

Hunting – Morland. 8.

Hunting Proverbs

SCENES/TITLES
1 'Stone walls do not a prison make'
2 'Nor iron bars a cage'

CHARACTERS
1 Man on horseback
2 Lady on horseback

PATTERN NUMBERS
D1534, D1535, D1536, D1931

BORDERS
Oak leaves with acorns

COLOURWAYS
Polychrome, blue and white

SHAPES
Flagon toilet set, unrecorded ice jug

DATES
This series was introduced in 1903. The date of withdrawal is not recorded but would have been before 1936

Hunting – The Quorn Hunt. Catalogue page. Top plate, features 1, teapots 3, cream 6, tea cup 7, sugar bowl 8.

Hunting Proverbs. *Above* 1, *below* 2.

Hunting – The Quorn Hunt

SCENES/TITLES
1 Two huntsmen, hats aloft
2 Huntsman jumping hedge with dogs and losing hat
3 Two huntsmen in foreground with group of three behind
4 Huntsman sounding horn
5 Huntsman followed by lady jumping fence
6 Dismounted huntsman calming horse of companion
7 Two huntsmen, one dismounted
8 Huntsman and child on horseback
9 Two huntsmen being served refreshments by a serving wench

PATTERN NUMBERS
D4468, D5051

COLOURWAYS
Polychrome

Hunting – The
Quorn Hunt.
Rack plate and
teapot, *left to right*
5, 2.

SHAPES

Rack plates, Quorn teaset, fern pot, teapot
stand, vase 7764, oatmeal saucer, fruit saucer,
clamp fitting tobacco jar, porridge plate, salad
bowl, Craig and Ancester ashtrays

DATES

This series was introduced in 1924, extended in
1930 and withdrawn by 1945

SPECIAL BACKSTAMP

Notes Many of these characters were taken from
the John Peel series and set in a different
background

Hunting – The Quorn Hunt. *Left* 9, *right* 4.

Hunting – silhouette. Fruit dish 1.

Hunting – Silhouette

SCENES/TITLES
1 Rear view of lady riding side saddle
2 Profile view of huntsman waving crop

PATTERN NUMBERS
D3042

COLOURWAYS
Holbein

SHAPES
Leeds round fruit dish, Tavern jug

DATES
This series was introduced in 1908. The date of withdrawal is not recorded although it would have been before 1936

Hunting – silhouette. *Above* 1, *below* 2.

Hunting – Simpson tea cup 10.

Hunting – Simpson. Plate 11.

Hunting – Simpson. Rack plates, *left to right above* 8, 9, 2, *centre* 3, 6, 7, *below* 4, 5, 1.

Hunting – Simpson. *Above* 12, *below* 14, 15.

Hunting – Simpson.
Above 16, *below,* 13.

Hunting – Simpson
SCENES/TITLES
  1 'Across the Moor'
  2 'Post and Rails'
  3 'In the Vale'
  4 'Gone to Ground'
  5 'Over the Grass'
  6 'Changing Horses'
  7 'Going to Covert'
  8 'The Master'
  9 'The Brook'
10 'A Hot Scent'
11 'The Meet'
12 'In Full Cry'
13 'The Road Home'
14 'In Kennel'
15 'Dog Fox'
16 Procession of huntsmen
17 Late additions to the series

PATTERN NUMBERS
D6184, D6185, D6186, D6231, D6326

COLOURWAYS
Polychrome

SHAPES
Stafford plate, beaker, fluted dish, teaplates,
Coupe, fruit saucer, oatmeal saucer, cream soup
cup and saucer, teacup and saucer, sauce boat
and stand, trays 7979, 8099, 8237, 8051A and
8015A, Octagon and square fruit dish, oval fruit
bowl, Devon comport, Winchester salad bowl

DATES
This series was introduced in 1947 and
withdrawn by 1960

DESIGNER
Charles Simpson

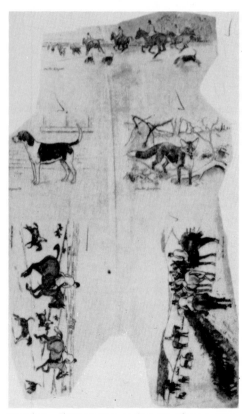

Hunting – Simpson (new series). 17. These scenes
were added later and may have been used, but no
titles are known.

Hunting – Thomson. A1.

Hunting – Thomson A
SCENES/TITLES
1 The meet, riders mounting
2 One lady and five gentlemen trotting
3 Lady and gentleman with little girl galloping
4 Two ladies and three gentlemen galloping

PATTERN NUMBERS
D1614, D2092, D2097, D2130, D2215, D2397, D2398, D2399

BORDERS
Stylised lilies, brocade, flowers and scroll, flower and feather brocade

COLOURWAYS
Polychrome, Whieldon

SHAPES
Rack plates, umbrella stand

DATES
This series was introduced in 1903 and the range added to until 1905. It was withdrawn by 1928

DESIGNER
Scenes 1 and 2 came from A 'Tally-Ho' Idyll drawn by Hugh Thomson which featured in the 1897 Pears Annual

Notes Scene 1 is also recorded divided into two scenes

Hunting – Thomson B
SCENES/TITLES
1 Horse caught on a fence, huntsman dismounted
2 Huntsman jumping a fence and losing his hat
3 Huntsman urging on his horse
4 Horse refusing a fence and huntsman falling off
5 Pair of huntsmen galloping
6 Huntsman galloping with hounds
7 Huntslady galloping

PATTERN NUMBERS
Not recorded

COLOURWAYS
Blue and white

SHAPES
Not recorded

DATES
This series features in a record book of 1925

DESIGNER
Hugh Thomson from the same source as series A

Hunting – Thomson. *Left to right, above* A3, A4, *below* A1, A2.

Hunting – Thomson. *Left to right, above* B1, B2, B3, B4, B5, *below* B6, B7.

Huntsmen at the Inn. Rack plate and jug, *left to right* 2, 3.

Huntsmen at the Inn. 1.

Huntsmen at the Inn

SCENES/TITLES
1 Huntsmen smoking and drinking at a steaming punch bowl
2 Huntsmen at a steaming punch bowl, one toasting and leaning on chair
3 Huntsmen smoking and drinking punch, one with his fist resting on the table

PATTERN NUMBERS
D2476, D2778, D2859, D2875

BORDERS
Leather bottle, foliate shell and scroll

COLOURWAYS
Polychrome

SHAPES
Rack plate, Clent jug, Virginia tobacco, 89 ashtray, unrecorded loving cup

DATES
This series was introduced in 1906 and withdrawn by 1928

DESIGNER
W Nunn

Gallant Fishers

SCENES/TITLES
1 'O the gallant fisher's life it is the best of any'
2 'And when the timrous trout I wait to take and he devours my bait'
3 'Of recreations there is none so free as fishing is alone'

127

Gallant Fishers. *Left to right* characters 5, 1.

Gallant Fishers. Rack plate and tray. *Left to right* Characters 6, 2.

Gallant Fishers. *Left to right, above* characters 4, 2, *below* 3.

CHARACTERS
1 Man on one knee fishing on the bank
2 A smiling man fishing cross legged on wall, his friend behind also fishing
3 Two sleeping fishermen back to back
4 Man lying reading beside man sitting on a chair fishing
5 Man sitting on a chair fishing
6 Two men fishing on wall, one glum, one smiling

PATTERN NUMBERS
D3680

BORDERS
Swallows

COLOURWAYS
Polychrome

SHAPES
Rack plates, Lennox flower bowl, Tudor jug, Crewe teaset, tobacco jar, York sandwich tray, Rheims teacup and saucer, vase number 7336, candlestick number 7667

DATES
This series was introduced in 1913 and withdrawn by 1936

SPECIAL BACKSTAMP

Golf. Rack plates and jug. *Left to right* 8, 4, 2.

Golf 5.

Golf. *Left to right* 3, 6, 7.

Golf

SCENES/TITLES
1 'Give losers leave to speak and winners to laugh'
2 'He that complains is never pitied'
3 'All fools are not knaves but all knaves are fools'
4 'He hath good judgement who relieth not wholly on his own'
5 'Every dog has his day and every man his hour'

CHARACTERS
1 Profile golfer choosing club from bag held by caddy
2 Putting scene with caddy blowing ball in
3 Golfer swinging, caddy holding flag
4 Golfer reading, caddy beside
5 Golfer putting, caddy standing by
6 Group of three golfers, one putting
7 Golfer with hands on hips, caddy behind
8 Golfer about to putt

PATTERN NUMBERS
D3394, D3395, D5960

BORDERS
Golf course

COLOURWAYS
Polychrome

SHAPES
Rack plates, Trophy (unrecorded), jug 7119, Westcott jug, stein, tobacco jar, tankard, Corinth jug

DATES
This series was introduced in 1911 and withdrawn by 1932

DESIGNER
Charles Crombie (fl. 1904–12)

129

Golf. Rack plate and jug. *Left to right* 1, 6.

The Nineteenth Hole.

The Nineteenth Hole
SCENES/TITLES
Two men drinking in front of the golf course

PATTERN NUMBERS
D3755, D3770

COLOURWAYS
Polychrome

SHAPES
Rack plate, barrel on stand

DATES
This series was introduced in 1914 and withdrawn by 1930

Old English Carnivals
SCENES/TITLES
1 Group led by girl with fan and gong player at rear approaching fruit seller
2 Group dancing to lute player and trumpeter
3 Group led by man playing squeeze box and girl at rear playing lute
4 Group led by man playing guitar, and another playing trumpet, little boy holding balloons
5 Group led by old lady with fan and man with hat raised
6 Group led by little boy with balloons, girls skipping and priest
7 Group led by boy playing squeeze box, little girl with balloons bringing up the rear
8 Group led by boy with balloons and squeeze box player bringing up the rear
9 Group led by guitar player and trumpeter bringing up the rear
10 Group led by squeeze box player and young girl with priest bringing up the rear

PATTERN NUMBERS
Not recorded

SHAPES
Not recorded

DATES
This series was featured in a record book of 1926

Old English Carnivals. *Left to right* 1, 2.

Old English Carnivals. *Left to right, above* 3, 4, 5, *centre* 8, 9, 10 *below* 6, 7.

Old English Country Fairs. *Above 5, below 7.*

Old English Country Fairs. 3.

Old English Country Fairs

SCENES/TITLES
1 Dancing around maypole – boy stumbling
2 Eleven people dancing around maypole
3 Boy climbing slippery pole
4 Three men tugging at yulelog, four watching
5 Wheelbarrow race
6 Dancing round the cattle drawn harvest waggon
7 Sack race
8 Peep Show
9 Bell ringing
10 Serving tea to soldiers
11 Scottish dancing
12 The Pig Race
13 The Roundabout
14 The Grand Bazaar
15 The Menagerie
16 Carrying the Guy
17 Football
18 Punch and Judy show
19 Hawker selling wares
20 Hawker with two baskets
21 Attendants bearing trophies.
Various incidental figures

PATTERN NUMBERS
D3470, D3541, D3611

BORDERS
Tree background or fair scene

COLOURWAYS
Polychrome, blue and white, Whieldon

SHAPES
Rack plate, Ball teaset, Concord jug, tobacco jar, spittoon, round salad bowl, Breda jug, Concord jug, Lennox bowl, Breda teapot, York sandwich tray, Joan teaset

DATES
This series was introduced in 1912 and withdrawn by 1928

DESIGNER
W Nunn

SPECIAL BACKSTAMPS
Michaelmas Fair, Mayday, Harvest Home, The Yulelog, Country Fair, Football

Old English Country Fairs. *Above*
12, *centre* 4, 6, *below* 2.

Old English Country Fairs. *Above* 14, *below* 19.

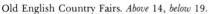

Old English
Country Fairs. *Above*
15, *below* 9.

Old English
Country Fairs.
Rack plates, *left
to right* 1, 18, 8.

Old English
Country Fairs.
Steins, *left to right*
17, 13.

Old English Country Fairs. *Left to right, above* 16, 10, *below* 11, 20, 21.

Scottish Hunting Scenes. Rack plates, *left to right* 1, 2, 3.

Scottish Hunting Scenes. 4.

Scottish Hunting Scenes

SCENES/TITLES
1 Hunter in kilt with dogs
2 Stag in rocky landscape
3 Retriever with game bird
4 Game birds

PATTERN NUMBERS
D3692, D3693, D3694, D3695

BORDERS
Chequered

COLOURWAYS
Polychrome

SHAPES
Rack plates

DATES
This series was introduced in 1913 and
withdrawn by 1928

DESIGNER
After designs by James Hardy (1832–1889)

Shooting and Archery. 1.

Shooting and Archery. 2.

Shooting and Archery

SCENES/TITLES
1 Shooting practice
2 Archery practice

PATTERN NUMBERS
D5058, D5062

SHAPES
Shaped rack plate

DATES
This series was introduced in 1930 and was
probably withdrawn during World War II

Skating

SCENES/TITLES
1 'Pryde goeth before a fall'
2 'Do not worry, do not flurry nothing good is
   got by worry'

CHARACTERS
1 Man and woman standing watching
2 Apprehensive skater, walking stick raised
3 Scared skater held up by another laughing
4 Skater with arms folded, three observers in
   background
5 Man and woman skating arm in arm
6 Unsteady skaters with arm up, one with
   cane, boy watching
7 Skater with duck walking stick back to back
   with another skater
8 Two unsteady skaters about to fall
9 Two skaters hand in hand, man chasing boy
   behind
10 Confident skater with cane in one hand
11 Two skaters chasing each other
12 Skater about to fall
13 Man and woman skating hand in hand
14 Skater balancing himself with cane.
   Various incidental onlookers

PATTERN NUMBERS
D2789, D2827, D2865, D2909, D3247

BORDERS
Greek key, skaters, wavy line, stylised leaves

COLOURWAYS
Polychrome, Holbein

SHAPES
Rack plates, jugs 7119 and 6061, Lennox bowl,
Concord jug, Breda teapot, vase 7023, Empire
cup and saucer, Mayfair toilet, unrecorded
vases, Athens teapot, ice jug, round salad bowl

DATES
This series was introduced in 1907 and
withdrawn by 1928

Skating. 9.

Skating. *Left to right* 7, 5.

Skating. Bowl, 10, 12.

Skating. Jug and bowl, *left to right* 11, 10, 2, 1.

Skating. Bowl and jug, *left to right* 6, 8.

Skating. Vase and plates, *left to right* 3, 4, 13. Greek key and skaters border.

Sporting Scenes. 1.

Sporting Scenes

SCENES/TITLES
1 'The Weary Sportsmen'
2 'The Benevolent Sportsmen'
3 'The Anglers Repast'

PATTERN NUMBERS
D5292, D5392, D5393

COLOURWAYS
Blue and white, sepia

SHAPES
Rack plate

DATES
This series was introduced in 1933. The date of withdrawal is not recorded

DESIGNER
After paintings by George Morland (1763–1804)

Sporting Scenes. Rack plates, *left to right* 2, 3.

Surfing. 1.

Surfing

SCENES/TITLES
A group of bathers at the waterside

PATTERN NUMBERS
D4645, D4789

BORDERS
Plain band, seagulls and clouds

COLOURWAYS
Polychrome

SHAPES
Rack plates, York sandwich tray, Quorn teaset, vase number 7538, Pitt jug

DATES
This series was introduced in 1926 and added to in 1928. It was withdrawn by 1942

Appendix

Since the publication of Volume One, a few interesting discoveries have been made in the following series:

Dickens (Volume 1, page 20/30)
Group A: an extra pattern number has been recorded, D3979, on a shaving mug
Group B: a new character, the *Punch and Judy Man*, has been found on a loving cup
Group D: These plates were based on illustrations by F. Barnard (1846-1896) which appeared in Dickens Household Edition
Group E: new characters have been found in this low relief series: *Bill Sykes*, *Old Peggotty* (two versions) *Sam Weller alone* and *Mrs Bloss with Mrs Tibbs*

Dickens E: Mrs Bloss and Mrs Tibbs from *The Boarding House* in *Sketches by Boz* 1836

Don Quixote (Volume I, page 32)
An extra pattern number has been recorded, D3120

Jackdaw Of Rheims (Volume I, page 38)
An extra pattern number has been recorded, D5689

Shakespeare (Volume 1, page 48)
Group E: Dogberry's Watch. The original watercolour for scene E2 has been found in a private collection
The missing quotation for E3 is: 'Dogberry first who think you the most disartless man to be constable'
The incidental background procession of watchmen has also been discovered as a teapot design D4167
A tankard, D4746, has also been found in the series

Dogberry's Watch teapot

Sir Roger De Coverley (Volume I, page 53)
This series was based on illustrations by Hugh Thomson which featured in the English Illustrated Magazine of 1885–6 and soon after in book form.

Castles and Churches (Volume I, page 83)
Several more castles have come to light:
    Ardencapel Castle D4643 and D4728
    Dunolly Castle D4643 and E7259
    Linlithgow Castle D4643
    Manstoke Castle D4357
    Richmond Castle D4643 and D4728
    Tintern Abbey D4643
Arundel Castle and Windsor Castle listed before are also both found with pattern numbers D4643 and Rochester Castle with number D5417

Shakespearean Characters (Volume I, page 51)
The series was still being sold in Australia in the 1930's so the withdrawal date of 1928 stated is a little early

Shakespeare's Country (Volume I, page 53)
Group 1: Two more scenes have been found by a collector: *Mary Arden's Cottage* and *The Memorial Theatre, Stratford*

sh Inns (Volume I, page 96/97)
 have been found in this series:
 Inn, Shanklin; The Talbot,
 ey Corbett; The Star, Alfriston; and
 hers, Ludlow

reton Hall (Volume I, page 97)
 a pattern number has been recorded
 l

d War I (Volume I, page 101)
 caption on the HMS Lion reads 'Our
 ous navy whose mighty power has held the
 for freedom'

 thanks to the following enthusiasts for
 ding us this information:

nald Austen	Doug Pinchin
e Bush	K J Shaw
m Kennay	John Shorter
orothy Mathews	David Swarbrick

Original Watercolour for Dogberry's Watch

The Crab Inn, Shanklin

Pattern and Code Numbers & Date Guide

The following tables of numbers indicate the approximate periods when the first relevant patterns so numbered were first *introduced*. Many patterns were in production over a number of years, carrying the same pattern number, and so the numbers cannot be used to establish the date of manufacture. This can be established either from the style of the backstamps, or from the impressed date code if present—normally the last two figures of the year preceded by a number indicating the month, for example 10.08 means a manufacturing date of October 1908. However, unless date codes are present, it is generally impossible to establish precise dates of manufacture for Series wares. In the tables below, A and D numbers indicate earthenware patterns, while E and H were used for fine china.

A Numbers

Pattern number	Date of introduction
1 – 6882	c. 1881 – 1892
6883 – 7467	1893
7468 – 8084	1894
8085 – 8592	1895
8593 – 9144	1896
9145 – 9617	1897
9618 – 10000	1898

D Numbers

Pattern number	Date of introduction
1 – 339	1899
340 – 769	1900
770 – 1137	1901
1138 – 1495	1902
1496 – 1869	1903
1870 – 2161	1904
2162 – 2442	1905
2443 – 2723	1906
2724 – 2914	1907
2915 – 3079	1908
3080 – 3229	1909
3230 – 3374	1910
3375 – 3519	1911
3520 – 3635	1912
3636 – 3714	1913
3715 – 3821	1914
3822 – 3939	1915
3940 – 4074	1916 – 1918
4075 – 4143	1919 – 1920
4144 – 4230	1921 – 1922
4231 – 4360	1923
4361 – 4470	1924
4471 – 4559	1925
4560 – 4659	1926
4660 – 4737	1927
4738 – 4822	1928
4823 – 4969	1929
4970 – 5069	1930
5070 – 5169	1931
5170 – 5230	1932
5231 – 5429	1933
5430 – 5520	1934
5521 – 5612	1935
5613 – 5749	1936
5750 – 5875	1937
5876 – 6009	1938
6010 – 6110	1939
6111 – 6285	1940 – 1948
6286 – 6390	1949 – 1952
6391 – 6408	1953
6409 – 6438	1954
6439 – 6454	1955
6455 – 6464	1956
6465 – 6492	1957
6493 – 6507	1958
6508 – 6547	1959
6548 – 6558	1960
6559 – 6567	1961
6568 – 6587	1962
6588 – 6596	1963
6597 – 6606	1964

E Numbers

Pattern number	Date of introduction
1 – 940	1901 – 1902
941 – 1950	1903
1951 – 3040	1904
3041 – 4054	1905 – 1906
4055 – 6015	1907 – 1910
6016 – 7863	1911
7684 – 8277	1912
8278 – 8933	1913
8934 – 9527	1914
9528 – 10000	1915

H Numbers

Pattern number	Date of information
1 – 359	1916
360 – 709	1917
710 – 759	1918
760 – 906	1919
907 – 1049	1920
1050 – 1179	1921
1180 – 1443	1922
1444 – 1812	1923
1813 – 2268	1924
2269 – 2649	1925
2650 – 3180	1926
3181 – 3599	1927
3600 – 3770	1928
3771 – 3909	1929
3910 – 4010	1930
4011 – 4099	1931
4100 – 4189	1932
4190 – 4240	1933
4241 – 4329	1934
4330 – 4425	1935
4426 – 4519	1936
4520 – 4609	1937
4610 – 4710	1938
4711 – 4821	1939 – 1942
4822 – 4849	1943 – 1946
4850 – 4906	1947 – 1952
4907 – 4930	1953
4931 – 4935	1954
4936 – 4941	1955
4942 – 4950	1956 – 1957
4951 – 4956	1958
4957 – 4959	1959
4960 – 4961	1960
4962 – 4968	1962
4969 – 4975	1963